TOO BIG to Ignore.
The Biggest Challenge Eve

TOO BIG to Simplify.
Embrace Complexity

TOO BIG for Our Systems.
Create a Free Place

TOO BIG to Go Alone.
Be Radically Inclusive

TOO BIG for Fragmentation.
The Power of Design

Act Now

Henk Ovink & Jelte Boeijenga

TOO BIG
Rebuild by Design: A Transformative
Approach to Climate Change

naioıo publishers, 2018

Contents

Rebuild by Design:
A Transformative Approach to
Climate Change
Introduction

On October 29, 2012, Hurricane Sandy slammed into the Northeast coast of the United States. Commentators called it a "superstorm"—a product of the hottest year in U.S. history, warmer-than-normal ocean surface temperatures, and a full moon that amplified the storm surge at high tide. Sandy measured more than a thousand miles across when it made landfall, hammering communities along the coast with winds of 80 miles per hour. The storm lingered, increasing its destructive impact. At least 186 people were killed, and damages exceeded $65 billion. More than 650,000 homes were damaged or destroyed, as were ports, water supplies, power grids, and generating stations. One of the world's iconic cities and America's most densely-populated coast were flooded. Sandy showed the world how vulnerable we all are. Many of us knew the risks but simply were not prepared for a storm of this magnitude. When the storm hit, there wasn't much to do but try to escape it.

"Tomorrow is going to be worse than yesterday" is not the story you want to tell your children or grandchildren. Yet every year, we pile record upon dismaying record. We read about, hear about, and experience higher temperatures, more carbon pollution, higher sea levels, more powerful storms, deeper droughts, diminishing forests and polar ice, more climate-related deaths, more climate conflicts and refugees, and on and on.

How do we transform such a world so that we make progress away from paralyzing risk and toward real achievements? How do we bring home this seemingly "too big" problem so that it is small enough to grasp? How do we understand it, see how to manage it, and act upon it? How do we get a grip on the problem politically, economically, and societally?

How, in other words, do we change the culture to deal with our increasingly complex future?

The challenges seem overwhelming. Today, humankind faces one of the greatest global challenges in history. After warming the planet for centuries, we now have only a matter of years to reverse course if we are to mitigate the damage caused by our actions. Meeting the objective of the 2015 Paris Agreement and limiting global warming to two degrees Celsius (preferably 1.5) will require an immense effort, in a short time, by everyone. The alteration that we have already brought about in the climate leaves very little room; the window for success is closing fast. We must make a massive switch to sustainable energy and drastically redesign our lives, economy, and culture. Even if we do everything we must, and limit the rise in global temperatures to two degrees, our path will be scattered with despair and destruction because climate change is not some abstract future concept. We will have to adapt to a changed climate no matter how effective we are at halting further global warming. Hurricane Sandy showed us as much. Climate change strikes with increasingly devastating force around the world on a daily basis, magnifying disastrous droughts, floods and storms and turning more people into climate refugees. Sandy wasn't the exception; Sandy was the announcement of a new standard.

While limiting global warming to two degrees Celsius might save humanity, some places already are past saving. Thanks to the combination of rising sea levels, urbanization, groundwater depletion and deforestation, many places are sinking and will go under. We have already lost too many lives. We will lose more as our planet and our economy are crushed under the inexorable pressures of an altered climate. We are not ready to face this. To minimize the effects of further warming, every place and everything has to change drastically. There is no choice to be had between energy transition and ending deforestation, between sustainable urbanization and building with nature, between a circular economy and planetary security. We do not have the luxury of choosing among these options, because they are not options. We have to do them all, and we have to do them now.

Sandy was a gripping, practical demonstration of what we understand theoretically: that major social, cultural, economic and environmental challenges are interdependent and interconnected. The hurricane magnified those interdependencies and connections. It became shockingly clear that the socially vulnerable also live in the most environmentally vulnerable places. In the poorer communities of New Jersey, the most fragile houses were the first to go. Those communities were not only flooded, they were also polluted as seawater surged through nearby industrial areas, gathering contaminants and pouring them into the surrounding neighborhoods. Moreover, the people who lack the money and the capacity to recover from a disaster like Sandy also are those hit the hardest. It all piles up: no home, no infrastructure, no electricity, no water, no drainage—just destruction, pollution and despair. What at first seems a natural catastrophe largely turns out to be a manmade disaster.

As the number and impact of climate-related crises grows around the world, so do these connections and interdependencies. More than half the world's population lives in cities, a share that is growing. Urbanization brings countries economic growth and prosperity, and often brings individuals social and economic emancipation. But cities, if not made resilient, are also where lives and property are at severe risk. Here, the consequences of climate change will be felt most forcefully. Here, all the complexity converges, for urbanization brings together issues of energy, food, ecology and society. Policy to address these connections grows from politics that should be informed by governments' ties to science and urban design and planning. Too often, though, policy makers do not have the tools to understand and make the most of the various interconnections.

There are no quick fixes in this situation, no silver bullets. A piecemeal approach of incidental fixes will fail, as it is insufficient to the challenges of complexity. To truly resolve the issues before us and prepare for an uncertain future, we must embrace that complexity. Complexity is the new normal. It challenges us to change, to seek real innovation, and thus to inspire coming generations. Complexity demands a new approach, one that steps outside existing frameworks and agreements based on assumptions made in the past. The act of turning boldly toward the future requires us to innovate, experiment, and use what we learn to actively change. We must free ourselves of too common "cannot," "must not" and "won't work" attitudes and embrace a "yes, we can" mentality. That, in turn, means we must set aside accepted roles and challenge longstanding relationships. We need coordination between the analysis of challenges and real understanding of them, developing a comprehensive perspective that connects us to immediate action and immediate impact. In other words, we need truly inclusive collaboration that ties everyone and everything, from the first day to the last, into a new working culture.

The day after the hurricane passed, President Barack Obama, a Democrat, walked the ravaged New Jersey shore with Republican Governor Chris Christie, witnesses to the devastation and despair. The following week, Obama was elected to his second term, and in December he signed an executive order creating the Hurricane Sandy Rebuilding Task Force. In Sandy, he saw an opportunity to advance his climate agenda, which had foundered in the Republican Congress, for Sandy made no distinction among political affiliations. In the immediate aftermath, the government's focus would be on reconstruction, putting $60 billion of federal money to work. His executive order directed twenty-three federal agencies, departments and offices to cut red tape and seek both immediate results and maximum impact during rebuilding. Sandy provided Obama with a now-or-never opportunity to put climate change front-and-center in the American political discourse, and he seized upon it in his second inaugural address in January of 2013.

Sandy was a personal disaster, affecting millions of lives. An effective response demanded tact and empathy—a human response from the president and his team. It also created an obligation: never again. Obama saw an opportunity to do things better tomorrow than they are done today. The responsibility to Sandy's victims and the obligation to prevent the same fate befalling other Americans in the future converged in the president's strategy. Obama's political instincts to seek cooperation, collaboration and innovation found expression in Rebuild by Design, which grew out of his initial executive order. This book chronicles the development and execution of Rebuild by Design, an unprecedented exercise in collaboration and innovative thinking at the federal level. In its first stage, Rebuild by Design resulted in the federal government investing $930 million to implement ground-breaking resilience projects, strengthening the places most affected by Sandy against the next inevitable consequence of climate change.

Rebuild by Design was, on its face, a design competition, but in reality, it was much more than that. Born out of a disaster, the competition was made possible by an ambitious president who felt an obligation to do better. Rebuild by Design was destined to make that radical change a reality.

For me, that change began in early January 2013 when Shaun Donovan, Obama's Secretary of Housing and Urban Development, stepped down from the train in Rotterdam, accompanied by his wife, Liza, and two young sons, Milo and Lucas. His appearance represented a last-minute detour on the way home from a family vacation. Shaun was the newly-appointed chair of Obama's Hurricane Sandy Rebuilding Task Force. He wanted to take advantage of his European trip to see what we in the Netherlands have been doing in the face of climate change. I, as acting Director General for Planning and Water Affairs of the Netherlands, had two days to show him everything relevant in terms of flood prevention, water protection, innovation, governance, finance, knowledge development and collaboration. We would have to move fast.

There was plenty to talk about. Shove a spade into Dutch soil and you will start a conversation about water. Every square meter of land is soaked in it; every place has a water story to tell. Twenty-six percent of the Netherlands lies below sea level, and 60 percent is vulnerable to flooding. Over time, we have built 3,000 polders—land we recaptured from rivers, lakes and the sea. The Dutch have made water great—in our politics, our culture and our waterworks. We are proud of our polder and our diking skills. Our cities are water cities, our democracy a water democracy.

Shaun was bursting with energy, eager to learn, and I was eager to be his guide. Racing across the country in a minivan, we bonded over new ideas, the fun of our mini-road trip and the urgency of the situation. In two short days, I crammed in all I could about the Netherlands' water culture, showing him what we had built and introducing him to the people who did the work of thinking about and dealing with water in the private sector, at research institutes and across all layers of government. I saw Sandy as a political and practical game-changer for the United States. Did Donovan perceive it the same way? The night he left, I asked him point-blank. Yes, he said. We agreed we would not let this opportunity go to waste. We felt a mutual ambition and shared obligation to take advantage of it, and I told Donovan I wanted to find a way to help. Global cooperation in the face of climate change is a no-brainer. We all understand that a water-secure world will be one in which we intensify our collaboration across the globe and change our strategies from response to preparedness.

What we built over the next two years was both a design competition that resulted in the commitment of almost a billion dollars of federal money and a conscious detour around the sometimes rigid and ineffective ways that government and the whole of society works. The winning projects that came out of Rebuild by Design were important, but there was another, lasting result. Rebuild by Design was not simply about making the best designs—nor was it only about building those designs. It was about changing culture. From the beginning, we were committed to breaking down silos in order to change the way governments address resiliency. In the end, over 500 organizations joined our collaborative quest to overcome the vulnerabilities and build upon the interdependencies of this incredibly diverse region. Rebuild by Design was an experiment for government, community groups, and the ten international teams of designers, engineers, researchers and scientists who joined with us. It was an experiment for philanthropic partners who dared invest startup funding into a new way of innovating within government. Everyone involved took risks based on trust. Many of those who participated in Rebuild by Design worked without the sense of control to which they were accustomed, without a certain outcome, and with immense creativity and ambition.

Rebuild by Design was purposefully "by design." At its core were design and the design approach, so familiar to us in The Netherlands. Our detour around existing-but-failing frameworks was only possible through the power of design, which has an unrivaled capacity to unify. A good design strategy integrates multiple challenges in a comprehensive approach. Design embodies the power to solve problems by considering the assets and the challenges at hand, by thinking across scales—from living room to city, from street to region, from coast to continent. Design also stretches across time, looking backward to analyze and forward to project how interventions will lead to impact. Good design doesn't just look at a road, for example, but also integrates the berm next to it, as well as the surrounding neighborhood and its social, environmental, economic and cultural needs. The process of design is opportunistic, inclusive and comprehensive, uniting people and places, addressing problems here and now with solutions that are feasible and workable. This last component of design would be critical for those of us working on Rebuild by Design, because we were continually aware that design is inherently political. Design can and should create a narrative that can seduce and convince people, informing and uniting them around complex decisions that lead to action. Design should be inspirational and aspirational, but we knew what we came up with also had to be something that could actually be accomplished inside the complex political ecosystem in which we operated.

President Obama has said that we are the first generation to feel the effects of climate change and the last that can do something about it. Hurricane Sandy was the disaster that provoked us into trying something different, and in that sense it was an opportunity. We do not need further disasters to generate further action, for we have never been as capable of meeting today's and tomorrow's challenges as we are now. Our knowledge and understanding of the future and our capacity to intervene and act have never been this great. Nor have the facts been this clear. We know the threat, we see the threat, we understand what can go wrong if we fail to act. We also can see the opportunities this threat gives us to work collectively for solutions, as we began to do through Rebuild by Design. This experience showed that collectively we have everything we need to think and act outside existing frameworks in embracing and grappling with a complex future. There is no reason not to act, and act now.

This book is my account of the story of Rebuild by Design, told through my eyes and those of many others. A collective voice shaped the culture of Rebuild by Design and is the culture of this book. This is a story of a competition, political dynamics, collaboration, research, and the design approach in action. I believe it is an important story because what we did—complete with its imperfections, improvisations and inevitable failures—is a harbinger of what all of us will need to do as climate change affects us. Our approach was rooted in embracing complexity and uncertainty because we believed doing so would produce better results, even though this was difficult for every one of us. Rebuild by Design was time-constrained, intense and often emotionally challenging. The projects that came out of it are exceptional, but they did not—and never could—make everyone happy. They were the result of a willingness by the players to put their cards on the table, trust where they used to hold back, collaborate where they were accustomed to competing and commit to real change in the way we worked. Rebuild by Design became seductive to those involved in it. We fell in love with it, and that love made all things possible.

I wrote this book to better understand that process, to learn from Rebuild by Design and inspire others to do the same. If I succeed, Rebuild by Design will be understood as a means and a method for change. Rebuild by Design is not a blueprint, as the circumstances—this region, that storm, that president—are unique. Yet I believe Rebuild by Design has set a precedent. It is possible to replicate and scale up its culture, and I hope that this book can inform and inspire others to do so—to take the next step, with the belief that they can do everything differently, every time.

I was able to develop Rebuild by Design thanks to President Obama, who wholeheartedly embraced the future and sought to make climate change a centerpiece of American politics; and thanks to Housing and Urban Development Secretary Shaun Donovan, who gave me the confidence to lead this experiment far beyond what we considered possible and guided me through the culture of American politics. I owe a deep debt of gratitude and love to my wife, Irené, who packed her bags and our eighteen-year-old cat, Alfa, to accompany me across the Atlantic and build life anew in D.C. Thanks also to Siebe Riedstra and Melanie Schultz van Haegen, Secretary General and Minister, respectively, of the Dutch Ministry of Infrastructure and the Environment and my superiors. They realized right away that the intersection of Hurricane Sandy with this moment in American culture was a golden opportunity for the Netherlands and the Dutch water approach. I am grateful also to Dr. Judith Rodin, president of The Rockefeller Foundation, who trusted Shaun and me and believed in a disruptive approach to transform our governmental systems. Thanks to the team at the Hurricane Sandy Rebuilding Task Force: Laurel Blatchford, Marion McFadden, Kevin Bush, Scott Davis, Irene Chang-Cimino, Josh Sawislak, Jamie Rubin, Holly Leicht, Ana Marie Argilagos, Stewart Sarkozy-Banoczy, Justin Scheid and all the other colleagues who dedicated their passion and professions to our collective work and believed against all odds that we could make this happen. Thanks to Amy Chester, who managed Rebuild by Design and steered it across the region, through all the politics, toward the best results. Thanks to Rebuild by Design's partners: Eric Klinenberg, Sam Carter, Tara Eisenberg, John Gendall, Daniel Cohen, Mary Rowe, Courtney Smith, Alexis Taylor, Rob Lane, Rob Pirani, Laura Tolkoff, Rob Freudenberg, Lucrecia Montmayor, David van der Leer, Jeff Byles, Jerome Chou, Lauren Altman and their teams. Their work was the backbone of Rebuild by Design, their dedication unprecedented. Thanks to Nancy Kete of The Rockefeller Foundation and all the other colleagues at the six philanthropic partners who believed in this promise and helped us deliver. Thanks to the Dutch Embassy in Washington D.C. and Dutch Consulate in New York. Their support for the teams and myself was critical and passionate. Thanks to the state and local governments of New York, New Jersey and Connecticut, and the schools, activists, businesses and many thousands of people in affected communities who engaged in this great experiment and put their trust in what we were doing. And of course, big thanks to the ten selected design teams, staff and partners. Their dedication was beyond expectations, their skills were magical, their capacity to engage was critical and their willingness to invest their hearts and minds were transformative.

Finally, I could not have written this book without the friendship, collaboration and passion of Jelte Boeijenga, who was willing to go through the whole process again with me. He helped turn my diary, notes, memories and thoughts into this story, and filled them out with extensive interviews with other individuals who played key roles. Because of the involvement of hundreds of organizations and thousands of people, Rebuild by Design has grown into a movement that illustrates that where there is a will there is a way, step by step, to really change the world. Yes, we can!

I wrote this book to honor my mother, Lies Ovink-Semmelink (1926–2011). She was hope personified, and her devotion to never leave anyone behind inspires me every day. She truly believed in people and in their capacity to always do good. This book is for everyone who has ever had the ambition to change the world. For everyone who believes deeply in people. For everyone with the will to get up every day and rediscover how to make collaborations work. Because we must. We can. And there is magic in doing so.

Henk Ovink
Rotterdam, December 2017

Editorial Note

In early 2015, Henk Ovink approached me with the idea to co-author "a book about Rebuild by Design—less about the projects themselves and much more about the process that helped develop them." He wanted the world to see what Rebuild by Design had accomplished in the wake of Hurricane Sandy. There had already been a lot of attention focused on the results of Rebuild by Design's international competition, a high-profile effort to build resiliency into the landscapes of New York and New Jersey. I had followed Rebuild by Design at a distance and seen how it had led, in a short time, to projects that could meaningfully alter the New York region's vulnerability to climate change. Moreover, these were not projects imposed on local governments and communities; they were owned and championed by them. Although I was not yet that familiar with Rebuild by Design's process, I sensed that it was something special. Its projects were major infrastructure investments in a densely populated urban environment that, rather than facing resistance from residents, had been embraced. They were not paper designs, either—in less than a year, almost a billion dollars of federal funding had been allocated to build the winners. The renderings and images shared with the world showed inspiring designs in urban planning and architecture. I recognized that these outcomes must be the result of a remarkable effort. Henk's invitation struck a chord, appealing to my personal interest and professional belief in the importance of showing that process to the world.

Henk wanted to make sure people understood the behind-the-scenes process that had brought about those results. "We must write a book about that process," he insisted, so that others might try something similar. His invitation was an easy one to accept. This was our challenge: how could Henk and I showcase this diverse, multifaceted process in all its intricacy? We wanted to tell the story of the research, the designs, the community struggles, the politics, the ambition and audacity of Rebuild by Design's approach, and the federal government's pivotal role. It was clear to us how unique the circumstances were: a disaster of unprecedented size; political commitment up to the highest level; the iconic appeal of the City of New York; and the extreme degree of capacity in the region itself. What did we want readers to learn from a process that was in so many ways unique—filled with improvisation and learning all along the way? Participants would later describe Rebuild by Design as "building an airplane while flying." Finally, how would we tell the story of something that is far from finished? After all, at the time of this writing there is little to show on the ground. Building the projects will take years, and replicating Rebuild by Design elsewhere may take decades.

As we began work on this book, it became clear how important personal commitment was in realizing Rebuild by Design. Many individuals who were essential to its success took some sort of risk—professional, political, financial. They believed in what Rebuild by Design was doing, and they found in it a home for their personal ambition and conviction to reconstruct the affected region better than it had been before. This personal commitment was evident among almost everyone I interviewed about their involvement in Rebuild by Design.

We realized, too, that the unique perspectives and commitments of many individuals are an important part of the story. If we were to write a book about this process, it would have to be informed by many personal perspectives. You will find in the following pages, interspersed within Henk's larger story and with his statements of his own vision, multiple private accounts of key individuals' experiences with Rebuild by Design—what they hoped for, what they expected and what they learned.

TOO BIG follows the timeline, as seen through Henk's eyes, of a twenty-three-month period from the end of October 2012 to September 2014. Part I describes Hurricane Sandy's impact on the Northeast coast of the United States and President Obama's response. Shaun Donovan, Secretary of Housing and Urban Development, tours the Netherlands with Henk, and both men recognize the extraordinary opportunity Sandy has provided to take a new approach to creating resiliency in the region. In Part II, Henk signs on to the effort and comes to the United States to organize what will be a very unusual design competition, one that challenges the federal system of funding big projects and threatens to overturn established ways of doing things. In Part III, the finalist teams are selected in the first round of the competition and a very nontraditional, highly-collaborative research stage commences. For two months, teams crisscross the region, both learning about the places and communities affected and building the political coalitions they will need to move forward. Part IV details the inclusive design process and the ongoing effort to remain ambitious and collaborative in the face of pressure to conform and compromise. Finally, Part V describes the judging and selection of winners and the awarding of funds—a process that was imperiled by politics even at that late stage.

Throughout this chronicle, our goal has been to reveal what it took to maintain a vision for a truly transformative approach to government and the creation of resiliency in the face of forces large and small that pulled toward old ways of doing things. Rebuild by Design succeeded not because it was the product of a single vision but because it was the joint effort of thousands. I interviewed over twenty key players, asking each about their agenda within Rebuild by Design and what was at stake for them, as well as their experiences, reflections and lessons learned. Their answers differ, yet from them a common picture emerges of a deep personal and collective commitment to make the world a better place. The sum of these ambitions drove the process forward and made Rebuild by Design what it is today.

We would like to thank all those who freely committed their time to answer our questions openly and honestly. Big thanks to so many who helped us shape and create this book and project. Thanks to George Brugmans, Adri Duivesteijn, Han Meyer and Dirk Sijmons for their valuable observations and critiques on earlier versions of this project and for the insight that this should be a personal book. Thanks to John Kirkpatrick for translating the Dutch manuscript into English and helping to sharpen our insight into what message we wanted to pass on. Thanks to Toon Koehorst and Jannetje in 't Veld for nourishing the process of creation and finding the perfect design for this book. Thanks to Rachel Sender for the beautiful portraits. Thanks to our publisher Eelco van Welie and nai010, who stayed with us during this entire expedition. Thanks to Jeff Goodell and Harlan "Hal" Clifford for their continuous advice and great work in editing and helping finalize this book in the best way possible.

And from me, of course, a big thank you to Henk Ovink for sharing this magical quest with me.

Jelte Boeijenga
Rotterdam, December 2017

PART I
Hurricane Sandy October 2012— February 2013

President Barack Obama and New Jersey Governor Chris Christie walk the Jersey Shore.

As Hurricane Sandy rages along the eastern seaboard of the United States, bearing down on New York City in late October 2012, I am glued to my iPad at home in the Netherlands. Through the screen, I witness the storm overwhelm the region, hitting New York front and center, taking scores of lives and causing massive damage.

On October 30, news cameras show Democratic President Barack Obama walking with Republican Governor Chris Christie along the shattered shore of Brigantine, New Jersey. Obama was in a tight race with Republican challenger Mitt Romney for re-election, the vote a week away. In the toxic atmosphere of the deeply partisan election battle, the scene was an unexpected and extraordinary one. Yet the president knew that now was not the time for political posturing. In 2009, he had promised, "No Katrina on my watch," and now he was going to prove it.

DEC 7, 2012.   THE WHITE HOUSE

Executive Order: Establishing the Hurricane Sandy Rebuilding Task Force.

"A disaster of Hurricane Sandy's magnitude merits a comprehensive and collaborative approach to the long-term rebuilding plans for this critical region and its infrastructure. Rebuilding efforts must address economic conditions and the region's aged infrastructure -- including its public housing, transportation systems, and utilities -- and identify the requirements and resources necessary to bring these systems to a more resilient condition given both current and future risks.

This order establishes the Hurricane Sandy Rebuilding Task Force (Task Force) to provide the coordination that is necessary to support these rebuilding objectives. In collaboration with the leadership provided through the National Disaster Recovery Framework (NDRF), the Task Force will identify opportunities for achieving rebuilding success, consistent with the NDRF's commitment to support economic vitality, enhance public health and safety, protect and enhance natural and manmade infrastructure, and ensure appropriate accountability. The Task Force will work to ensure that the Federal Government continues to provide appropriate resources to support affected State, local, and tribal communities to improve the region's resilience, health, and prosperity by building for the future." [...]

President Barack Obama

Sandy was not a Democrats' or Republicans' storm. It was a human disaster that took 168 lives and caused tens of billions of dollars in damage. Obama's presence on the ground wasn't symbolic. True to his faith, his beliefs and his ambition to make America better and more just, he committed to Christie and the American people that he would deliver fast, effective aid. Following his re-election, he turned his attention to the opportunity Sandy presented to create a rare bipartisan moment in Washington. He began with an executive order creating the Hurricane Sandy Rebuilding Task Force, charged with cutting red tape and getting things done. Obama knew he had to provide first aid and disaster response to those communities hit hardest, while also looking ahead toward rebuilding better than before.

Sandy played a prominent role in his January inaugural address to Congress, underscoring his argument that the effects of climate change do not distinguish between Democrats and Republicans. Over Christmas, Obama had pushed a $10 billion emergency aid bill through a Congress that had initially failed to approve his $60 billion relief package, twisting arms to make it happen. Now, Obama wanted the rest. Later that winter, Congress would provide the remaining $50 billion in Sandy recovery funds that Obama had requested initially. Obama would marshal his administration to turn the reality of climate change into effective political action by collaborating across the region and across the political divide. When a crisis hits, Americans stand united, and Obama was determined to make the most of the moment.

Living With Water

It was a sponge in the shape of the Netherlands that made everything click for Shaun Donovan. The U.S. Secretary of Housing and Urban Development (HUD), newly named

HUD

Klaus Jacob
Interview p.102

"The right people were at the right time at the right place. And that's important. That's why elections are important, that's why the political process is important."

The sand engine (Zandmotor) off the Delfland Coast, the Netherlands

chair of Obama's Hurricane Sandy Rebuilding Task Force, saw this tourist trinket when we toured the Maeslant storm surge barrier in Rotterdam. He and his family had arrived in Rotterdam on January 2, tacking a brief stop onto the end of a vacation to Berlin, Germany. A man of intense curiosity, he wanted to learn about how the Netherlands handles water. As acting Director General for Planning and Water Affairs, it's my job to show him everything the Netherlands has to offer in terms of water management. We have a minivan, a driver, and 32 hours.

We start in the City of Rotterdam, then head for the Maeslant storm surge barrier, Deltares in Delft, the sand engine (Zandmotor) off the Delfland Coast, Scheveningen Boulevard, Amsterdam and the new flood resilient North-South metro link. We meet the staff of our Deltaprogram, visit the Rijkswaterstaat knowledge center in Lelystad and the inflatable dam (Balgstuw) at Ramspol, see the citizen-operated flood protection in Kampen and meet with the Regional Water Authority.

We race across the country, from the houseboat in Amsterdam where he insists on staying (aggravating his security detail), to city and town, beach and office. Yet it is the souvenir sponge that stands as his metaphor for the Netherlands, a culture literally steeped in water; a nation that has wrested most of its land from the sea and negotiates its relationship with water every day. I come to understand Shaun

29

as a man determined to get things done—deeply political, cognizant of the differences between what I am showing him in the Netherlands and the political and social culture in the United States.

This trip reveals to me an alignment of factors that create a once-in-a-lifetime opportunity. First, Sandy—a deadly and devastating storm in America's most densely populated region, striking at the heart of the largest and most iconic American city—illustrates how vulnerable all of us are to the consequences of climate change. Second, Obama is an ambitious president in his final term, determined to use the federal government as a force for good to help not only repair the damage but prepare for a climate-challenged future. Obama ran on hope and change, and I believe he is capable of delivering so much more, despite the evident disconnect between Capitol Hill and much of the rest of America. Then there is America's can-do culture, marked by ambition and an entrepreneurial mentality. Finally, Shaun Donovan appreciates the Netherlands' centuries-long experience living with water. We are world leaders in water management—experienced, successful and proud. Here is an opportunity for us to step up and show the world, on a very public stage, what we can do. If we can make the rebuilding of New York and New Jersey a showcase of resiliency, we will not only change those places, but we will set a new global standard for climate resiliency, adaptation and innovation, as well.

Donovan and I hit it off from the moment we step into the van, and as I get to know him I see that he is the perfect man to lead the Hurricane Sandy Rebuilding Task Force. Born and raised in New York, he served as housing commissioner under New York Mayor Michael Bloomberg before joining Obama's cabinet as HUD secretary, and he is close to the president. A Harvard graduate with degrees in architecture and public administration, he is enthusiastic, ambitious, dedicated and very, very smart. He chairs the task force and will control a quarter of the $60 billion in federal relief funds. I am certain he has the character,

HURRICANE SANDY BY THE NUMBERS

· At least 159 fatalities

· 650,000 homes damaged or destroyed

· $65 billion in damages and economic loss

· 200,000 small business closures due to damage or power outages

· 2 million working days lost

· 70 National Parks impacted

· 100 million gallons of raw sewage released in Hewlett Bay two days after Sandy

Hurricane Sandy Rebuilding Strategy: Stronger Communities, A Resilient Region, Hurricane Sandy Rebuilding Task Force, August 2013.

the capacity and the opportunity to create real change—to set a new standard for how governments respond to disaster and prepare more effectively for the future.

After I say goodbye to Shaun and his family, who will spend one more night on their Amsterdam houseboat before flying home, I sit with my wife, Irené, and share my thoughts. I feel a burning ambition to step into this opportunity. We discuss everything, turning over the possibilities of what I see as a once-in-a-lifetime moment. I want to go to America. I want to help. As Donovan wings across the Atlantic, I write him an email. "Dear Shaun, I think Hurricane Sandy can be a game changer for the United States. If you agree, I'd love to work with you." I stare at the screen for a moment, then add, "I hope I'm not being too forward."

The next day, I have a response in my inbox, one Shaun typed on his phone as his plane taxied to the international arrivals terminal at Dulles: "You're being just forward enough."

Despair, Destruction and Opportunities

I land in New York in February 2013 to follow up on written recommendations I made to Donovan after his visit. Donovan's task force has established teams in Washington, New York and New Jersey, comprising staff from the federal government, states and cities. They take me out to see for myself what, until now, I have only experienced from afar. More than three months after the storm, the region is still afflicted by wrecked houses, burnt-out neighborhoods, collapsed walls, destroyed wastewater plants and other effects of widespread flooding.

At Coney Island, along the southern tip of Brooklyn, the project manager of the U.S. Army Corps of Engineers proudly shows us how he is rebuilding the floodwall to the precise specifications of the one that was destroyed. His plans date back to the 1990s and make no accommodation for climate change or sea level rise. I quickly discover that, for many people in the United States, there is no such thing as climate change or a rising sea. These are not subjects you talk about in polite company. If I bring them up, they laugh or deflect the question, or deny the science. The Coney Island floodwall

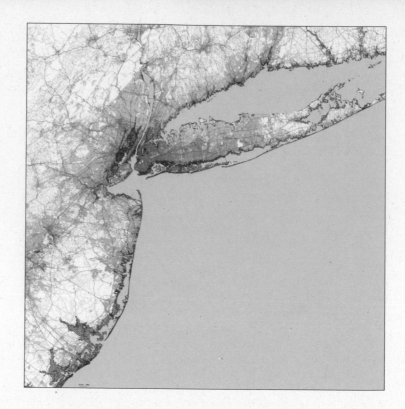

Extent of the storm surge of Hurricane Sandy

illustrates the nature of our challenge. It will be insane to pump billions of dollars into repairs that only meet obsolete data and standards. If we want to make Sandy the climate-preparedness game changer it should be, we have to get our heads around the denial that affects so much American political discourse on the subject. How can we use their doubts to bring about change? I know the answer does not lie in forcing unpleasant realities down doubters' throats. But if we can get them to the table, we will have a chance to work together toward aware-ness, understanding and insight.

Dawn Zimmer
Interview p.166

"Unfortunately in this country there remains a huge misunderstanding. Even in Hoboken—even though 80% of our city was under water—there are residents that feel like: Well, we just had a hundred-year storm, so that means we won't have anything for another hundred years."

TOO BIG
to Ignore

The Biggest Challenge Ever

The Biggest Challenge Ever

"We are now in truly uncharted territory," said World Climate Research Program Director David Carlson at the release of <u>World Meteorological Organization</u>'s ⁻ w m O climate change report in March 2017. Coming from one of the world's most fact-based organizations, "uncharted territory" means serious trouble. And the WMO is not alone. Climate change is increasingly visible, increasingly irreversible and increasingly significant to people all over the world. Like a diabolical magnifying glass, a warming climate enlarges the force and frequency of storms, lengthens the periods of droughts and swells human misery as millions lose their possessions, jobs, friends and families. These changes destabilize communities and regions as harvests are lost and wells go dry. We can see the effects of climate change at the root of growing poverty, unrest and even war in many regions. Climate refugees are not some <u>dystopian</u> future concept; they are a growing reality, driven across borders by drought, flood, conflict and despair. Global warming threatens our cities, our natural environments, our food supplies and our economies. As we recklessly deplete natural groundwater supplies, cities sink because of soil subsidence. This worsens the effects of saltwater encroachment. The dramatic increase in sea level rise drowns deltas and erodes islands. Climate change threatens the lives of billions of people and puts trillions of dollars of assets at risk. If we continue down this road, an extraordinary 40 percent of the world's population will have been devastated before 2080 from too much water, or too little. X

The Biggest Challenge Ever

On December 12, 2015, governments, businesses, academia and NGOs gathered at COP21 agreed that enough was enough. With the Paris agreement, we put a stake in the ground and pledged to take action to keep the climate from warming by more than two degrees Celsius. That agreement was historic, but it didn't change culture. Nor could it. We cannot change our ways of working, our governance, our laws and regulations, our organizations and our procedures with a stroke of the pen. But if we are going to do what we collectively said we would do, all of those elements of society will have to change. It is part of human nature that we turn our eyes toward the future yet dwell in the past, considering ourselves to be limited by existing frameworks and conditions. Our solutions respond to past disasters rather than prepare us for the future. And while we know everything is interconnected, we still spend our money in silos and hesitate to work together. After the heady flush of a conference and the ceremony of a formal agreement like COP21, we fall back into old patterns. Distrust and existing power structures reassert themselves, creating standoffs between governments and their constituencies, between people and science, between those most affected by the disasters and those responsible for creating them. What is our pledge worth if we lack the processes, the investments and the approach to make that promised action a reality?

The Biggest Challenge Ever

We have no time to waste. Each day of indecision means
more despair, more disasters and less time to mitigate
and adapt. Mitigation means holding global warming to
the maximum-agreed two degrees Celsius, thus keeping
the damage to a manageable level. Adaptation entails
safeguarding the many places that are threatened even
under this two degree goal. To deliver on the Paris pledge,
we must radically change the way we live and work. We
must embrace our future's complexity, not deny it. We
cannot simply work on incrementally better plans and
solutions because what we have been doing has not
delivered the results we need. We must dare to make a
different start, with different assumptions and different
processes to seed a true change in our culture. This
demands an inclusive approach—with and by everyone—in
which we dare to confront the full complexity of society
with a comprehensive response. We must truly believe
in the human capacity to understand, collaborate and
intervene. Yes, we can—we can act with our hearts and
minds aligned, focused on that challenging future, with
true ownership, out of responsibility and with the ambition
and guts to really change the world.

"Whether it's government making the investment or private sector or philanthropy, to get a single outcome for a single investment is not something we ought to be accepting in the 21st century. Nobody has enough money to do that."

Judith Rodin
Interview p.90

The Sandy Task Force has three objectives. First, provide effective, coordinated aid to everyone in need throughout the region. Second, as fast as possible, repair the elements of critical infrastructure: hospitals, water provision and sanitation, roads and energy supplies. Third, rebuild. It is in this third objective that we face a key choice: either copy and paste from the past or think differently to create future-proof solutions. We either respond to Sandy (fight the last war) or we prepare ourselves for an uncertain and potentially worse future (imagine the next war). Here, then, is the big opportunity, the reason I wanted to come to America.

"The statutes as they were on the books practically allowed rebuilding to only what was there before. Because how do you decide if something is an improvement towards resilience instead of accommodation of personal needs? So it was simple: you rebuild, but not beyond. From a bureaucratic point of view that's fabulous, from a resilience point of view it's a total disaster."

Klaus Jacob
Interview p.102

The situation before us is a classic "wicked problem," characterized by contradictory information and opinions, vast numbers of people involved, a massive economic consequence and deep, poorly understood interconnections with other problems. It's exactly what I want to grapple with. What if we invest the Sandy funding in creating the necessary new perspective? What would it mean for us today, for how we work here and now, if we could imagine that uncertain future and work back in time? I am convinced that, if we do this collectively, we can be innovative and comprehensive in ways that propel recovery work forward. And the New York region—so bold, innovative, progressive and dynamic—is the best place to try. The ground here is fertile for experimentation. We have more than an opportunity—we have an obligation to show the effects of coming climate change, to show how the region is so tightly interdependent on managing those effects, and to propose solutions that truly address the magnitude and complexity of the necessary work. If our analysis is truly thorough, if it is comprehensive and inclusive, we can identify the most important vulnerabilities and the greatest opportunities. Then we can rebuild this region in a way that is transformative—not only on the ground, but in how we work to solve these hardest of problems.

Innovation and Comprehensive Investments

Right after his January visit to the Netherlands, I wrote Shaun two reports: one on the scope and governance of the task force, the other on innovation. We had to figure out how to simulate Dutch-style innovation using existing American legal frameworks. Shaun felt we could take advantage of the America Competes Act, which is designed to stimulate innovation. We would figure out the most pressing problems and ask the free market to help us solve them. It was clear, however, that we faced something of a round-peg-square-hole problem. That legislation was not written to address the kind of collaborative innovation I knew was necessary. We didn't yet know what went wrong when Sandy turned the region upside down and inside out. To figure out the problems and the opportunities, we needed to develop a design competition that was collaborative and inclusive, rather than competitive. That was how we were going to get to the best outcomes—by asking design competitors to learn and innovate together.

This approach comes from my Dutch experience with planning and design. The long-term Randstad 2040 vision, the way we partner with the International Architecture Biennale in Rotterdam, the design approach we developed for the Olympic Plan, Room for the River, the Coastal Weak Link program, the Deltaprogram, the Architecture Policies for that matter—all are examples of this Dutch design-driven, collaborative approach. We are driven by the goals of seeking safety and quality for our economy, society, culture and environment. My challenge would be to translate this Dutch way of doing things into a workable model for Donovan and the task force.

In my report on governance, I identified several interconnected opportunities. Most of the $60 billion in federal relief funds would be spent on infrastructure repair: water and waste systems, roads, power grids, rail lines and so on. But the funding was siloed into the budgets of different agencies. Fragmentation of funding leads to fragmentation of work and a lot of missed opportunities and inefficiency. On the other hand, when everything needs attention, there is an opportunity to take a comprehensive approach, not only to seek efficiencies but also to build better than before. And this approach has the potential to stick—to last beyond the recovery from this disaster, reshaping the way institutions and individuals work across lines.

A design approach requires tackling all the recovery challenges and competing demands comprehensively, place by place. Additionally, we could seize opportunities to add value through this comprehensive approach, so that the places where we work are actually improved and better prepared for the future. And we

"Rebuild by Design asked for flexibility in many, many ways. It was about funding flexibility; it was about jurisdictional flexibility, it involved thinking differently about how you spend the money and how you look at returns in the future. It involved different relationships with local players. For all of the great things that Rebuild by Design did, you had to set the conditions for. When I came into the administration in early 2009, the economic crisis was in full swing and the American Re-investment and Recovery Act was just passing through Congress, with close to 800 billion dollars of emergency assistance. One of the things that we learned from that experience was: how do you move money quickly through non-traditional channels and agencies without running into all kinds of problems, in a world of Congress and inspector generals who almost want to see you make a mistake? So even if you assume that there's a desire to do good, how do you keep an eye on that over time without constricting people's ability to be flexible where they need to be? That's a hard line to walk. One of the things I set up

Laurel Blatchford

Chief of Staff of the U.S. Department of Housing and Urban Development (HUD) from 2009 to 2013 and Executive Director of the Hurricane Sandy Rebuilding Task Force from January to September 2013

on the task force was a project management office—a capacity to track and manage funds. It was about being accountable and transparent to the principles that we set forward for how the recovery money was going to be spent. It was a big, maybe less sexy or visible, but still important step towards creating shared accountability. And that's a foundation for innovation too. If you have willingness to communicate and trust among the agencies, when they know that their basic management and oversight needs are being met, that allows you to be more creative."

could exploit efficiencies, saving time and money and avoiding frustration. In order to take advantage of all of this potential, we had to begin with understanding. We needed deep and thorough analysis to, first, unravel the way things went wrong across the region and throughout all the overlaid, interlocking jurisdictions, and second, understand what resources we have, how to organize them, and how to invest them. Getting this right was going to take time, attention and energy. And it was essential to everything that would follow.

This Is America

After my early February tour of New York and New Jersey, I take the train to Washington D.C. to meet with Donovan and his team in his office in the HUD building. The structure was designed by the Brutalist architect Marcel Breuer, and Donovan's beautiful, severe office remains true to the original design. It's clear that the two reports I sent to Shaun the month prior have had an impact, and we quickly get into details about how they are approaching reconstruction, the hurdles they face, and next steps. As the meeting is wrapping up, Donovan asks everyone to leave the room except me and Laurel Blatchford,

Marion McFadden
Interview p.54

"The first thing you ask when you think of a competition is: what's the problem we're solving and what's the prize? With Rebuild by Design we said: we're not going to tell you the problem, you're going to define the problem."

executive director of the task force. I know what's coming, and I'm ready for it. He looks me in the eye. "Do you want to join President Obama's Hurricane Sandy Rebuilding Task Force?"

The question is a formality. He knows I do. I walk out of the building and call Irené back in The Hague in the Netherlands. I am exhilarated and convinced. Are we really going to pack up and move to D.C. in a few weeks? Yes, she is ready to do it, and so am I. I call my superiors at the Dutch Ministry of Infrastructure and the Environment, Melanie Schultz van Haegen and Siebe Riedstra, Minister and Secretary General, respectively. They need no convincing. We want to show the world that preparing for the future together is both an opportunity and a necessity. No one doubts that whatever the personal and professional challenges, this is the right thing to do.

As "Henk from the Netherlands," I roll up my sleeves and join the work with Laurel Blatchford, Marion McFadden, Kevin Bush, Scott Davis, Josh Sawislak and the rest of the task force team. They welcome me in with a "let's get to work!" attitude. The atmosphere is suffused with ambition, collaboration, political pressure and, especially, urgency. Extreme urgency. From the moment Congress appropriated an additional $50 billion to the Sandy recovery effort in February of 2013, the task force had a mere six months to draft a complete rebuilding strategy and allocate the money. Some of my colleagues are under 30 but are veterans of bitter political fights on Capitol Hill or in the trenches of Obama's two presidential campaigns. Their grit and commitment is impressive. My sidekick Kevin Bush is a "Presidential Management Fellow." In the Netherlands we'd call him a trainee, but it wouldn't have the same ring. He works for the president and is deeply proud of that. Everyone here is. They are on Obama's team, and they don't want to let the president down. The Hurricane Sandy Relief Bill demands that the task force come up with a complete rebuilding strategy that will allocate $60 billion in six months. We must spend the money as effectively as possible on housing, infrastructure, policy changes, insurance and so on. There is no time to waste.

The task force is an interagency team, built by borrowing individuals from different parts of the government to join working groups. One of the first things I learn is that, in America, building organizations starts with people, rather than structure. Leverage comes from one's network—who you know, what their power is, what they are like to work with, what you think they can get done. Structure comes later.

The procedures we deal with, though, remain daunting. The government's insistence on sticking with an old procedure for creating "concurrence," is surprising. Typically, different agencies work on projects in silos. The White House oversees those agencies and then makes sure everything is in alignment—this is "concurrence," and it creates a very top-down power structure in which agencies stick to their own silos, missing the interlinkages, crossovers and advantages of collaboration. Our approach is to build the task force from different agencies plus the White House, with Shaun heading it up and all of us working closely day and night. Since the collaboration is inclusive, and everyone who needs to be represented is, then there should be no need for the old concurrence review by the White House. After all, everyone agreed and signed off—including the White House itself! But existing powers insist on continuing the concurrence process nevertheless.

Another challenge for me was our inability to institutionalize what we were learning. Sometimes in a meeting, someone would respond to a suggestion with "been there, done that." I realized I wanted the lessons of our collaborations to be documented and available to others in government. The task force process we were developing was a good example of collaboration, and it should be shared. We drafted language with the task force team "to evaluate the task force process, approach and procedures, and use that evaluation for federal government improvement." I was astonished to see this language dropped from the final report. How, I wondered in the face of that amazement, can we learn ourselves? How can we improve, not only what is on the ground but also the institutions that support society? How do we mix this dedicated approach with increased institutional capacity and reform?

Whether to build the task force around procedures or around powerful people isn't really the question. After all, there are plenty of places where the rigidity of procedures doom government organizations to ineffectiveness, and I am here in part because I see an opportunity to break away from established ways of doing things (when procedures determine the fate of the planet, we will all be in trouble). What matters is the outcome: how can we use the task force both to take advantage of the wealth of experience and capacity of its members, and also use it as an educational mechanism, a means toward better government? The solution lies in flexibility and adaptability. We will learn as we go, borrowing from the old way of doing things when that makes sense, trying new things as much as possible, testing, failing, succeeding, learning and testing again.

SHAUN DONOVAN–"Winners and losers create competition, and often bring out the best in people: they strive, they bring new ideas that they wouldn't otherwise bring. And you're able to spend money to do something to a depth or a scale that you're not able to if everybody just gets a little piece. So it can become comprehensive, it can become a beacon or a shining example. It shows a way, a path to something that is stronger."

Shaun Donovan

Secretary of the U.S. Department of Housing and Urban Development (HUD) from 2009 to 2014 and Chair of the Hurricane Sandy Rebuilding Task Force.

JELTE BOEIJENGA   Where did Rebuild by Design start for you?

SHAUN DONOVAN   There are different ways I could answer that. I am trained as an architect, and a big believer that competitions that bring together different perspectives and professions can be a powerful way to spark innovation. I think that was something I understood from a longer-term perspective beginning with a number of experiences early in my education and my career. When I was housing commissioner in New York City, I put together a competition called New Housing New York that brought together architects, landscape architects, sociologists, developers and others, a very broad range of perspectives. That is perhaps the best example of what I had done before, that really tried to employ this idea of multiple perspectives, both in the competing teams and in the jury, to create innovation. I've always thought about these competitions as driving innovation where the result can be a kind of beacon or flagship. Not with the idea that every single project that follows can live up to that level of quality, but it becomes an example which then filters through other work more broadly.

JB   And then also raises the bar?

SD   That raises the bar for the winning project and that raises the bar for everything. It's interesting–I remember one developer who did a lot of affordable housing in New York who sat on the jury and became very interested in hiring better architects for his projects in the future. So it can happen in ways that you don't necessarily anticipate or expect in advance. I also felt strongly that you see many competitions that are competitions of ideas: New Housing New York was intended to be, and ultimately ended up being, a competition of real projects. Of making things. The competition ended up being quite successful and we built the winning design.

> **"We knew there would be a lot of aid that would be spread, not by competition, but by need. And that needs to happen: you would never want 100% of the relief to go through a competition."**

And then of course there's the other way I could answer your question. I was asked by the President to lead the Sandy Rebuilding Task Force and I was planning a trip with my family to go visit friends of ours in Berlin for New Year's. I had heard many times from Judy Rodin, from people in New Orleans, from my friends Mitch and Mary Landrieu, about the partnership with the Dutch in the work they were doing in Louisiana. So I'd been quite interested in the Netherlands, and I decided, much to the chagrin of my two young boys, that we were going to take part of our family's New Year holiday to go look at flood protection measures in the Netherlands. We actually rented a houseboat in Amsterdam and we ended up being shuttled around on a bus for two or three days with Henk Ovink as our tour guide.

As we were traveling to look at infrastructure, "Room for the River", flood protection, Henk and I began talking about this idea of an international design competition that might advance innovation, not just for the U.S. but for the world, in thinking about flood protection, not just as infrastructure, but as something that was much more than flood protection, as something that could stitch together communities, that could enhance things as broad as arts and culture and recreation. We began really thinking about how to make that competition a reality. And I thought it was a very interesting conversation, but only a conversation.

On my way home, I had just begun to think about how I could put any of this to work with the Sandy Rebuilding Task Force, when we landed back in the United States at Dulles Airport. I turned on my BlackBerry and there was an email from Henk. It said: I hope I'm not being too forward, but I'd like to come work with you on Sandy. And I remember being stunned enough that I showed it to my wife and I said am I reading this correctly? We were both very excited, and that really began the process of us working together. I've often said to him: you were exactly forward enough! Meaning that if he hadn't taken that step, everything that would come afterwards wouldn't have happened. He needed to be that forward.

JB   A year ago, you said a competition doesn't only have winners but also losers and that there's nothing more difficult for government than that. Especially after a crisis. You knew this, you knew there would also be losers in the end. What made you still decide to do this competition?

SD   We knew there would be a lot of aid that would be spread, not by competition, but by need. And that needs to happen: you would never want 100% of the relief to go through a competition. But the political imperative, and I mean that in the formal "big P" political sense, but also the "small p" political sense when people are just interacting, leads to everybody getting a piece. The easiest political thing to do is to spread it like peanut butter, because nobody has grounds to complain. The problem is that it tends to be less effective. Both because winners and losers create competition, and often bring out the best in people: they strive, they bring new ideas that they wouldn't otherwise bring, and also because you do something at scale: you build an entire thing.

"Picking, choosing, making heavy investments and big bets in certain things can pay big dividends."

You're able to spend money to do something to a depth or a scale that you're not able to if everybody just gets a little piece. So it can become comprehensive, it can become a beacon or a shining example, even if not everything else that gets done can be at that quality. It shows a way, a path to something that is stronger.

I come from a background of housing and community development. One of the hardest things for anyone to do is pick certain neighborhoods over others. But the way the process of revitalization happens in a city is often that a particular neighborhood starts to change for the better, and that then spreads. It's not that everything starts to improve at once. That experience certainly taught me that picking, choosing, making heavy investments and big bets in certain things, often at the expense of political repercussions, is something that can pay big dividends. And with Rebuild by Design we always understood that a relatively small piece—a billion dollars is not small, but out of a total of over 60 billion dollars of aid it was still just a piece—could be very, very powerful if done in the right way.

> ## "I always remember the President saying: 'We ought to get this out to our local supporters.'"

Henk and I started to talk about this very early on. What we understood is that we needed strong alignment and political support within the administration. And that support was tested. The fact that I was the secretary and I wanted to do this gave Henk the ability within HUD to break some eggs, to push the boundaries. But Rebuild by Design and the awarding of the dollars, the CDBG-DR funds, remained separate and distinct throughout the whole process. When I said to Henk and the people that were competing "we will be able to award money, we will build these proposals," I couldn't 100% promise it, but they needed to trust me. I knew HUD had never done anything like that before, and that other parts of the federal government would need to support the process when we started picking winners and losers. So I spent a lot of time with people in the White House, getting them up to speed, helping them understand and build excitement in the White House for it, including with the President. I remember we were on Air Force One together, and I took some time to explain to him the competition, what we were doing, and I always remember him saying: "We ought to find a way to get this out to many of our local supporters, because this isn't necessarily something that a lot of people in Congress or in Washington would understand, but people that supported me from the beginning, that work in communities, would understand this." I think it was only once or twice that we needed to go to him, when the resistance was particularly strong, but building that support in the White House, including from the President, was quite important for withstanding what we knew would be political resistance to saying well, don't use the money for that. Use it to just...

JB   Spread it like peanut butter?

SD   Well, peanut butter is... I want to be clear. There were real tensions, right? There were risks that this money could take away from people who needed to rebuild their homes. So it's not without risk. We had to fully believe in what we were doing. I also needed to be convinced, and I was, that there was enough money for really doing what was necessary. Not everything that everybody would have wanted, but enough to reach people whose incomes were low, who really needed the money. And that was important to me, that we did the math. I was relentless and my team was relentless in looking at those needs and trying to be fair about it.

> ## "It's not without risk. We had to fully believe in what we were doing."

JB   The selection of the winners was in your hands. In your hands only, actually. But there was also a professional jury who advised you on the quality of the proposals. How did you reconcile these two realms? The design world on the one hand, in which the quality of the proposal is defined in pro-fessional terms, and the realm of politics in which you might want to select a project not because it's so good from a purely professional point of view, but out of political reasons: because it would be really good if it were to happen.

SD   My experience with these kind of problems, or challenges–I don't know if I would even call it a problem, it's reality, and in some ways it's healthy tension–my experience is that the best way to attack challenges like that, in life in general, is to bring both sides of that challenge together and let each side own the challenges that the other is feeling. And what I mean by that is we tried to be transparent that there were constraints like that. For example, we wanted to have geographic diversity in the winners. And that's good for politics but I think it's also good to have types of examples in different places. For the losers, who might not have won funding in the competition, but are interested in moving forward and have examples nearby, it creates momentum that is spread throughout the region. Also, one of the things that we did was to retain the flexibility to give smaller grants for planning, where we might say: look, there's a lot that's good, even it's not a winning design. Often the process itself of people working together in the competition leads to new ideas and projects, even if you can never predict precisely where these processes will go. In other words, through the planning grant, we were giving them the ability to go and do more.

    We tried to frame all of that in the competition and bring the professionals on the jury into those tensions, have those discussions, and have them own them as well. And we brought people onto the jury, not just me, who understood those tensions. And to your question about having sole determination, I wanted to make sure that my thinking was as transparent as possible because it really was shaped by the jury. Ultimately I didn't deviate from what the jury wanted; my decision-making was made stronger and better by both the jury itself and the conversations that happened there. And also these projects don't exist in a vacuum. So understanding what the politics are potentially puts you in a place where you have a better chance of success. So rather than saying design and politics are completely separate, or design judgment is good and political judgment is bad, they're both reality and we brought them together in the conversations.

> **"The support that we built, from the President on down, allowed us to make decisions that weren't necessarily going to be the easiest political choices. "**

But ultimately, we took into account the single most important thing, which was the quality of the proposals. And the support that we built, from the President on down, allowed us to make decisions that weren't necessarily going to be the easiest political choices. And look, that sometimes required tense conversations with the political leadership, with Chris Christie, with Andrew Cuomo, with Bill de Blasio and their teams. And we had those conversations. We wouldn't have picked Hoboken, for example, if we wanted to avoid politics. I think having politics inform the process in the right way, but not own the process or drive the process, is what we aimed to do.

It reminds me that one of the hallmarks of Rebuild by Design, one of the things I give Henk most credit for and that was different from New Housing New York and other competitions, is there was a lot more uncertainty about what we would get in the end. And that made it even more difficult on the politics. I think in every case, creativity depends on an exploration without a known end. If you're going to create something new, by definition you can't know, when you start, what it's going to be. I don't believe in the idea of the light bulb going off and a new idea being conceived fully formed by an individual author. It is by definition a messier, more iterative, more collaborative process than that. But with New Housing New York we at least knew what we were asking for: here was the site, and then within those bounds, creativity was unleashed. So there was some uncertainty there, but at least we could say: we're going to get 200 apartments. It was more concrete, literally and figuratively. Rebuild by Design was a much broader playing field. The process that we intentionally set up for Rebuild by

Design was a process of research to get to the competition itself. In that way it made our jobs more difficult, but also led to more interesting results. I remember the presentations for the jury and the amazing diversity and passion in the groups presenting: that never would have happened without a deep investment in community building and research. That was a real leap of faith that was a very important part of the competition. A leap into the unknown that compounded the challenges we had in terms of matching design quality with politics. To help everyone reach for a result that no one would have expected when they started, in a way that I think was quite powerful. For me it distinguishes Rebuild by Design not only from New Housing New York, but from most competitions that I've seen.

"You're building that capital in your relationships when the sun is shining"

JB   Your leadership is being praised–again and again–as being pivotal for making Rebuild by Design happen. What is that leadership? What does it take to be a leader?

SD   Building trust is enormously important. Henk and I built trust pretty quickly. But it was also really important that I had the trust of people at HUD and within the administration. I would say this to people who are working on something complicated: in those moments where it's hard, what

you are drawing on is the capital that you've built when the work isn't hard. And that's the trust, right? It's like every week you're putting a little bit of money aside into an account. You're building that capital in your relationships when the sun is shining, so when something goes wrong and an elected official is screaming at the White House, the people sitting across the table say: Okay, I trust you, Shaun, I've worked with you enough, I know what your intentions are. It's knowing that you've built capital, so that you can draw on it in a moment when you really need it.

The flip side of that is making sure that people who work for you know that when they're taking risks, if something goes wrong, which it inevitably will when you're trying something new, that not only am I not going to scream and yell at them, but I will have their backs and I will go to people in the White House and say that was my decision, it's not their fault. I always remember a time I screwed something up in New York City when I was housing commissioner and I got a call on my cellphone, directly from Mayor Bloomberg. He asked me to talk him through what had happened and why I made the decision, and at the end of my explanation, when he knew I had tried to do the right thing for the right reason, he said, "Do it again." That was when I knew that he trusted me. So that's a really important part of leadership, certainly at HUD and in the public sector more broadly, which is an environment where it's very hard to take risks, because everything we do is scrutinized. As long as you're taking risks for the right reason, if you're not failing, you're not taking enough risk.

Of course it's important knowing when not to take risks: being able to figure out where you should go out on a limb and where you shouldn't. There were times where Henk pushed me and I said no, I can't do that, or we shouldn't do that; we might win the battle but lose the war on that. But at other times program officials or lawyers told me I shouldn't do this–this is too risky or this is a problem–and I felt strongly that it was worth doing. So I said we're going to do it anyway. Leadership is knowing when not to take those leaps, but most leaders, particularly in the public sector, don't leap enough.

JB To what extent can you say that Rebuild by Design led to change within the federal government?

SD I think it is part of what has been a much broader change in the way the federal government approaches resilience. This *not under Trump!* was what the Sandy Rebuilding Task Force really focused on, and Rebuild by Design was one element. We've just taken important steps in updating the way the entire federal government operates taking into account future flood risk. Rebuild by Design was part of the momentum for doing that. I also think HUD and other agencies are more open to these kinds of competitive processes. It has added to the momentum for using competition to drive innovation.

And, it's interesting, I think it changed people. There were a range of folks who told me the Sandy Task Force and Rebuild by Design changed their careers. One example is the woman who was the deputy director for the rebuilding task force, who had been a lawyer at HUD. This was her first policy opportunity. After watching Rebuild by Design come together, watching the risks that we took and the way they came out, I think she would say she grew more both in her interests and also her capacity, her capacity for risk-taking, her capacity for creativity, for thinking differently about how to do things. It's the hardest to quantify in some ways, but it could ultimately be the most powerful, that you change the people within the federal government whose capacity is to then create more innovation in other realms.

The last thing I would say is perhaps the most obvious, which is that Rebuild by Design is not just history, it is living. It is being replicated in many other communities, in the U.S. and around the world. The power of an idea is that it can be replicated and begin to change other governments, change other places. I think that's the most powerful kind of innovation, if something can escape theory or philosophy, to become self-perpetuating. I give Rockefeller a lot of credit for seeing that potential in Rebuild by Design and adopting it and bringing it into their resilience work.

▲

MARION MCFADDEN–"The driving force behind innovation is that we all want to see it done better. And the whole concept was: you get everyone in the room to talk about their needs, their ideas, talk about what's going wrong and what it could look like. And getting to the best thing. People can differ on what exactly is required, but these projects really struck the chord of making the place more enjoyable, not just as a flood protective matter, but making the place better every day."

Marion McFadden

Chief Operating Officer and later Executive Director of the Hurricane Sandy Rebuilding Task Force in 2013.

JELTE BOEIJENGA You were the attorney for HUD during the setup of Rebuild by Design. What did it take to make this competition happen?

MARION MCFADDEN The first thing you ask when you think of a competition is: what's the problem we're solving and what's the prize? With Rebuild by Design we said: we're not going to tell you the problem, you're going to define the problem. And: we give you a small amount of money that might be just enough to cover your costs. After that, maybe, some day you will be chosen, subject to someone else's procurement laws. What? This asked for creativity at every turn. On the legal side, but also in setting up the competition itself. We had a joke at HUD: we find the "no" in innovation. We were not known for being really creative and forward thinking. When we were setting up the Hurricane Sandy Rebuilding Task Force and first talked about this idea of a design competition, this was one of 16 priorities. And this was the one that kept me up at night.

JB Can you describe the opportunity Rebuild by Design presented for the federal government?

MMF After Hurricane Sandy we were conscious of how slow and challenging the Hurricane Sandy recovery process was. And we were directed by the President immediately to rally all the resources of the federal government to support the affected jurisdiction. We were quick to realize that there was going to be tens of billions of dollars or more for infrastructure work in the region. The federal government is broken into different agencies that have statutory mandates for what they're to do. For example, the Army Corps of Engineers has very specific instructions from Congress about which beaches to replenish and which other projects to do. At HUD we don't have that kind of direction on our money, so we've been fairly hands-off about the selection of projects after disasters. And here we realized we had a real opportunity to shape how some of the money would be spent.

"We had a joke at HUD: we find the "no" in innovation."

But HUD itself lacked expertise in infrastructure work. So as a part of designing the process, we turned to the rest of the federal agencies. And they were mostly thrilled. We had an amount that hadn't been determined, but it was probably going to be a billion dollars or more, that's what it looked like. And who wouldn't want a chance to influence how someone else's money gets spent? So we had more than a dozen agencies represented in creating the request for qualifications, the design brief for the teams. We had evaluators from across the federal government so that we made sure we had the best in the field to assess the quality of the teams. We also had support from the President; we had the Hurricane Sandy Rebuilding Task Force, comprised of members of the President's cabinet. And later we had quarterly meetings at the White House organized by the OMB director or the President's representatives to pull it together. So it was a high-level project, it had prestige, it was a lot of money and it was meaningful.

> "When CNN.com declared Rebuild by Design the first of ten big innovations in 2013, all of a sudden that little bit of extra validation helped people warm up to the idea."

JB   And the grantees, did they also see that opportunity straight away?

MMF   If we had gone to New York State, New York City, Connecticut and New Jersey immediately after Sandy and said we want you to compete for funding and a design competition, this wouldn't have worked. They would've said no, we just had a catastrophic disaster, we don't have time for this, we're not going to engage in this. We didn't ask them, but that's my guess. When we told them we were doing this, they didn't embrace it warmly right away. Because they were overwhelmed with need. Immediate housing needs, clearing out the debris and

all the kinds of emergencies to get back on their feet. They weren't thinking long-term recovery yet when we got going on the design competition.

JB   And what made them embrace it in the end?

MMF   It was a slow process over time of showing them that nobody was trying to build something in their jurisdiction that they didn't want. It wasn't the federal government building. We weren't putting money into the hands of private companies or non-profits or whatever. Rockefeller wasn't making the decisions. But they didn't know that in the beginning. They were used to the formula block grant: "You give us the money, we choose from a menu of activities and as long as it's within the rules, you let us do it. You're suddenly exerting a different level of control that is uncomfortable, at a time when we're overwhelmed."
But over time they saw that the projects were really beyond what they would have done. I think one of the most helpful things was when CNN.com declared Rebuild by Design the first of ten big innovations in 2013, the CNN Ten. And all of a sudden that little bit of extra validation helped people warm up to the idea. All of a sudden it was something special that was happening, something newsworthy. Not just the federal government meddling or being overly bureaucratic.

JB   To what extent was the money and the possibility of real impact the driving force behind the competition?

MMF   What is the driving force behind innovation? The driving force behind innovation is that we all want to see it done better. If we can, we want to do better. And the whole concept was: you get all the right people in the room, all of them, an inclusive process. Get everyone in to talk about their needs, their ideas, talk about what's going wrong and what it could look like. And getting to the best thing. People can differ on what exactly is required, but these projects are beloved. They really struck the chord of making the place more enjoyable, not just as a flood protective matter, but making the place better every day. That was the driver. Did knowing how much money we had have a huge influence? Absolutely, something was going to get built. That's what we were starting from, let's get in there and make sure that the best minds are focused on what it's going to be.

like APL decision making ✗

"The President himself was setting the example. He said: we're going to do better than the last time we had a terrible storm."

JB   What will be the lasting effect of Rebuild by Design?

MMF   Let me acknowledge that the President himself was setting

the example. The President of the nation said: we're going to do better than the last time we had a terrible storm. The person he tasked with running the effort, Shaun Donovan, had a close relationship with the head of a major foundation, which brought a lot of money to the table. And then you had a region that was so populous and of so much interest to so many people. Those are unique circumstances that may not be repeated. It would be a different experience to try and do something in a more rural area, for example. So I don't know that it will exactly replicate itself, but it certainly left a mark within the federal government. And Rebuild by Design showed that great things can happen after disasters. We used to say: there are no wins in disaster recovery. The best you can do is "not do poorly;" there is always more need and people don't recognize the successes. And it's hard, hard work. So it's hard to shine in that kind of situation. But here we took something really noteworthy. That left a mark within the federal government.

JB   A mark, within people, or also within the institutions?

MMF   With people. The law hasn't been changed. There isn't a permanent structure resulting, but there is nothing permanent about the way the federal government handles disaster recovery. It changes every time, because there is no standing legal authority. Congress just writes a law after the worst disasters. But once you build relationships, you can't forget them. Once people influence the way you think, it's there for good. The HUD employees now know people at many other agencies. So if there is a question about environmental protection or transportation or whatever, they know someone at that agency to talk to. We were so used to being in our own small areas. And Rebuild by Design made us get more comfortable with guiding the grantees. Saying this is what you *should* do, these are the questions that you *should* ask. Instead of being hands-off, taking on more of a leader role. In the context of the block grant program where HUD distributes money by formula to 1,200 jurisdictions nationwide, it makes sense to say: you know your area better than I know it, so choose from the menu and it's up to you. But the federal government has more expertise in disasters than local jurisdictions do. So here it makes sense that they push harder. They're investing so much money in one place that they have a greater stewardship responsibility, to make sure everyone's making better choices. I think that is a sense that is carried through, that I saw in my staff. They obtained that greater comfort level.

"Once you build relationships, you can't forget them. Once people influence the way you think, it's there for good."

And, eventually, politics has changed. I remember, at the time, some members of the U.S. House of Representatives questioned and voiced concern about our emphasis on resilience in the Sandy work funded with CDBG. It was politically unpopular. At one point, when we were diligently describing our plans to ensure that Sandy requirements would make communities stronger and safer, a frustrated House staffer laid her head on the table and uttered "I wish you'd stop saying that!" What was common-sense to us struck them as expensive and just plain too hard. Rebuild by Design and its progeny, the National Disaster Resilience Competition, had to be vigorously defended against the notion that they would make recovery too expensive and time-consuming. But this year, in the House report to the 2017 funding bill for HUD, the appropriations committee for the first time took a stand in favor of rebuilding in a more resilient way. So I think both competitions ultimately helped Members of Congress see the value in investing in resilience measures.

▲

MARION MCFADDEN–"Rebuild by Design showed that great things can happen after disasters. We used to say: there are no wins in disaster recovery. The best you can do is "not do poorly;" there is always more need and people don't recognize the successes. And it's hard, hard work. So it's hard to shine in that kind of situation. But here we took something really noteworthy. That left a mark within the federal government."

PART II
Developing the Competition March—June 2013

We Don't Know the Real Problems

In 2011, President Obama reauthorized the America Competes Act, the legal umbrella under which we will hold the design competition that we are developing. The White House Office of Science and Technology Policy (OSTP) is interested in using competitions and design challenges to address societal problems, but I want to go beyond the typical approach. The need for this becomes apparent in a day-long Resiliency Incentive Prize Workshop in New York, chaired by Nancy Kete of The Rockefeller Foundation. Representatives from the U.S. Department of Housing and Urban Design (HUD), the White House, OSTP, The Rockefeller Foundation, the city of New York and the states of New York and New Jersey fill the room.

There's a lot of intellectual firepower in the meeting, but I leave believing we are not thinking in truly transformative ways. We spend the day talking about what we know and coming up with solutions—for example, rebuilding the electrical system around smart grids. That's a good idea, but we

OSTP

aren't digging deep enough. We come up with solutions but they aren't sufficient. They must be deeper, more engaged, directed at the wicked problems. We need to grapple with the connections and interdependencies, with the mix of needs and opportunities to prepare for climate change and an uncertain future. Real resilience comes from understanding the people involved and the challenges they face. Good design thinking demands starting from a position of asking questions rather than posing solutions. Proposing a smart grid or an intelligent dike is insufficient. We must grapple with the truly wicked problem of resilience by touching the ground, hearts and minds of a region that is home to millions of people and dozens of governments—a region that not only must recover from the recent hurricane but which must expect similar or worse climate-driven catastrophes in the future.

Sandy showed that thinking of solutions in isolation will not accomplish this. All issues—ecological, economic, social and cultural—mesh together, but our collective thinking at the Resiliency Prize Incentive Workshop does not reflect a true awareness of this. As far as I can tell, no one seems able to step back and really grapple with the complexity. The capacity to do that isn't there, and there is pressure to get to work on the ground. Understandably, people are dealing with their own challenges, trying to move their work forward and deliver visible results for their communities and constituencies who have been affected by Sandy. I can see that this way of working—focused on doing something and doing it fast—limits their impact and capacity for long-term change. The way they are working, the way they are thinking, will not be transformative.

If we truly wish to create resiliency, to be better prepared the next time around, we have to change the way we work together. I know this in my bones. I know that we have to go beyond seeking a holistic understanding of the region and

"The communities are the people who live there. They really understand the nuances of the environment and the context. The great ideas don't only come when a group of experts sits around at a conference table and thinks them up."

Judith Rodin
Interview p.90

its needs to rethinking the different roles and responsibilities of various components of government, society and non-profit institutions. If, as we scope the design competition, we limit ourselves to calling for proposals that address known problems, we will squander the opportunity Sandy presented to shake things up and think differently. I will have come to America for nothing.

A truly design-centered approach to solving problems has to begin with understanding them deeply, and we're not doing that yet. The only approach that will work is for everyone involved to immerse themselves in the communities and stakeholders throughout the region—not to tell them our answers but to ask them questions about their needs, their challenges and the opportunities for change. That means this "competition" must really be a force for collaboration. We can't swoop down on the communities at risk with "solutions." Rather, the competition must embrace an extensive, inclusive process of mutual discovery that brings together scientists, researchers, politicians, designers, communities and governments, cutting across lines of scale and lines of political convictions.

Scott Davis

Senior Advisor to the Office of the Secretary at the U.S. Department of Housing and Urban Development (HUD) till 2017 and Senior Advisor to the Hurricane Sandy Rebuilding Task Force in 2013

"We were looking to innovate from a policy perspective, from a design perspective and from a community engagement perspective as well. We wanted to get the community involved from the beginning, both in defining the problem and developing the solution. So instead of the designers coming up with their solution and the public approving of it, we wanted the community to be really engaged in an iterative participatory process, going back and forth and back and forth to arrive at the design. It gives them ownership and also builds up a certain level of accountability within the system. Because the public will expect more of the implementing government, whether it's the state or the city. Once the federal government's hands are off, the community can say, 'No, we've been involved all this time. These are our expectations, we voted for you and we're going to hold you accountable.' To develop that level of ownership, community buy-in and longer-term accountability, that's really important. If you invest in that process in the beginning, it pays off in the end."

√ I envision a multi-stage process that begins with a collaboration between local and global talent to conduct an in-depth analysis of the region's interdependencies and challenges. From this research, we will select the best opportunities to do impactful work, then create strong alliances to design solutions. Everything must have buy-in and support, across the board. This must be the culture of Rebuild by Design.

I also want to change the role that government usually plays. Rather than going to the market during the bid process and saying, in effect, "Here, you solve this wicked problem," I want the federal government to position itself within the coalition as a team member that owns the problem, deeply understands it, and stands by a commitment to help deliver a solution. This approach is how we are going to learn from the rebuilding effort—not only how to fix the problems on the ground, but how to work in fundamentally different ways that reflect the demands that climate change is making on all of us. This is why I am here. This is what I meant when I wrote to Shaun that Sandy is a game-changer. Rebuild by Design will not be a competition; it will be a quest to discover what can make the region more resilient and the world a better place.

It Takes Millions to Spend Billions Right

When I wrote my first advisory reports in January of 2013, I had no idea I would ever be in this position, working in the U.S, let alone how much support and leeway I would have in

"Rebuild by Design brought forward that you need all these disciplines: you need a sociologist, you need a designer, you need an engineer, you need the community activist, you need different stakeholders. Individually, they all have a certain trained reaction to problems that are not going to be sufficient to solve the problems that we're facing. And collaborating–people were able to overcome individual professional vulnerability and weakness. For everybody to acknowledge what they know and that they don't know what somebody else might know, is a huge leap forward for community development."

Carlos Martin

Senior Fellow at the
Urban Institute

my role as senior advisor to do what I envisioned. I soon found out: what I could do ultimately depended on Shaun Donovan. He is patient and keeps his temper (most of the time), but he is also determined. And he is all in. Donovan embraces my vision for Rebuild by Design, and as soon as he does, things move fast. From day one, the core idea of Rebuild by Design is to devote a share of the federal funds to innovative, future-proof solutions for the region. Obama had asked Congress for $60 billion in December, but the first funding bill allocated only $9.7 billion. This money went to immediate response. In February, Congress—pressured by the president and representatives from the affected states—revisited the request and allocated an additional $50 billion. Of that $50 billion, Donovan's Department of Housing and Urban Development has control over $15 billion: the Community Development Block Grant for Disaster Recovery (CDBG-DR). Rebuild by Design, Donovan tells me, will get a portion of that and may have as much as $1 billion to work with.

CDBG-DR

Before we can award that money and put shovels in the ground, we have to organize the competition, and there is no federal funding for that. All the CDBG-DR funds must go to the affected states and cities, who will ultimately implement the projects we select. Nor do we have the time to wait through another budget cycle, as we must be ready to commence work within a year, when the third and final tranche of rebuilding funds will become available. Otherwise, that money will end up somewhere else. I do some quick calculations to figure out how much we'll need to run the competition. If we expect sizable teams working for nine months, would $50,000 for each team be enough? No. A hundred thousand for each stage? Maybe. There is never enough, but more is impossible. Competitors are going to have to put skin in the game, and even then, with ten teams, we would need two million dollars. I estimate another two million to organize and run the research, collaboration and design process. I must find at least four million dollars—who can help?

The American federal system is built this way on purpose. Responsibilities are local and regional, so federal funding is directed to states and cities, who decide how to spend it. I am trying to work within the rules but also bend them. My vision is that, through Rebuild by Design, the federal government will guide that spending more directly. We will host a design process that the other players can't or won't—a process of collaboration—and in so doing, we will collectively come up with the best solutions that the states and cities should then implement. In my experience, investing in the process up front leads to better outcomes. We must spend millions to spend the billions right. But this approach, in which the feds take a more aggressive lead in determining how the money will be spent, is not part of American culture. We could not force it, yet I was convinced we needed it.

Infrastructure Resilience Guidelines

The biggest chunk of federal aid from the Sandy bill—more than $40 billion—is allocated for infrastructure and divided among several federal agencies and departments. The most important are the Department of Housing and Urban Development ($15 billion), the Department of Transportation

"Never before have we told the state or the local government, 'Here's what you're going to build,' let alone 'Here's who you're going to hire to build it.' Traditionally after a disaster, the federal government assists state and local government by giving them grant money with the large understanding that they know their problems best. So we make allocations based on damage estimates, and the grantees are expected to define what their priorities are. 'You had 70 percent damage? You get 70 percent of the money. Tell us what you want to do with it. As long as you can reflect that it corresponds to the impacts. And we'll only push back if you put the money where your friends are, instead of the damage.' So the system is state- and local-driven. We're the federal government; we don't own the land and we don't have any jurisdiction to decide what happens. And the big change of Rebuild by Design was that the federal government did want to exert influence on how the grant money would be spent. This meant we had to create a design process that would make the project so attractive that state and local

Scott Davis

Senior Advisor to the Office of the Secretary at the U.S. Department of Housing and Urban Development (HUD) till 2017 and Senior Advisor to the Hurricane Sandy Rebuilding Task Force in 2013

government would want to build it. We couldn't force it on the mayors and the governors, so we had to make sure that the design teams came up with a project that was consistent with their priorities. We couldn't make them build it; all we could do was say, 'If you build that, we'll give you this big pile of money.' And that's harder to say no to. Especially when you have everybody else in the community saying, 'We really want that.' So we didn't have the stick, but we were able to dangle a big carrot."

(DOT, $12.5 billion), the Department of Homeland Security / Federal Emergency Management Agency (FEMA, $11.5 billion) and the U.S. Army Corps of Engineers ($5 billion). The federal government in America is no different from its foreign counterparts in being neatly organized into sectors that tend to operate in their own silos. (I am introduced to the term "Balkanized" as a descriptor.) So each department or agency visits the region on its own. One deals with roads, another railways, the next water, dikes, energy, waste, whatever.

DOT
FEMA

Imagine you're the mayor of a small coastal town in New Jersey brought to a standstill by Hurricane Sandy. You face problems with sewage management, roads, electrical grids and gas pipelines. Representatives of each of these agencies come by. They all have money. If you want some of it, you need to provide a plan for recovery and projects to spend it. You must repeat this process for each agency or department. You can see the disaster after the disaster beginning to unfold. Even if, despite limited capacity, you manage to produce strong agreements between the federal government, state and your town to build good projects—a road, a dam, a drain, a park—you know there is a high risk of failure. All those projects must go through the permitting process simultaneously, your citizens must understand and support them one by one and then they have to actually be built. There is a very high risk of a lock-in, stalling implementation, probably with high failure costs. By addressing your town's needs separately, you miss the opportunity to combine and integrate them, to get projects to influence each other positively and complete them more intelligently, to save money and time and add value. You miss opportunities for greater impact in terms of acceptance and synergy, opportunities for new solutions and true innovation.

I know that if Rebuild by Design can break down the institutional silos around the funding agencies, we will set the stage for a more holistic, effective approach. To be able to connect the dots, we first need to know what we are talking about, and we must possess the desire to work together for a comprehensive approach that will produce transformative results.

The task force decides to give it a try. Together with the Army Corps of Engineers, we organize a workshop with all the agencies, the states of New York and New Jersey, and New York City to develop infrastructure resilience guidelines. These will inform how all of the task force's spending is allocated, not simply the work of Rebuild by Design. We invite all the players, but everyone is focused on the risks of this approach, not on the opportunities. They fear slowing down, fear losing their autonomy, fear compromising on their own agenda. No one wants to put all cards on the table. Who really believes in this, in joining forces? Maybe no one at all. Still, we want to see what happens.

My task force colleague Josh Sawislak is in charge, together with colleagues from the Army Corps of Engineers. We gather a list of six thousand projects that need funding; analyzing their interdependencies, we identify some 300 that are heavily dependent on each other. I suggest we map them—literally put them on the map by their geographic coordinates—to show the spatial implications of their interdependencies. Where demands and solutions pile up, workshop participants can see the overlap and the implied opportunities for coordination, combination and efficiency. Our intent in the workshop is to examine one place at a time, analyzing projects in terms of independencies (where do they converge, spatially and physically), management (who is in charge of what), funding (where do the different sources of finance converge) and scope (to what extent there are shared or conflicting interests between mobility, economy, housing, ecology, water and so on). Naively, we believe we can consider many of the 300 projects in a single day; in the end, we cover only a handful. Still, I am pleased by the results. The overlaps spark the right

AUG, 2013.   HURRICANE SANDY
REBUILDING TASK FORCE

Infrastructure Resilience Guidelines

Comprehensive analysis: Use comprehensive, forward-looking, and science-based analysis when selecting, prioritizing, implementing, and maintaining infrastructure investments.
Transparent and inclusive decision processes: Select projects using transparent, consistent, and inclusive processes.
Regional resilience: Work collaboratively with partners across all levels of governance and the private sector to promote a regional and cross-jurisdictional approach to resilience.
Long-term efficacy and fiscal sustainability: For all infrastructure programs, agencies should require a plan to monitor and evaluate the efficacy and sustainability of the implemented project.
Environmentally sustainable and innovative solutions: Ensure that Federal infrastructure investments align with the commitment expressed in the President's Climate Action Plan
Targeted financial incentives: Implement meaningful financial incentives and/or funding requirements to promote the incorporation of resilience and risk mitigation into infrastructure projects.
Adherence to resilience performance standards: Collaborate with State, local, Tribal, and territorial governments, as well as private stakeholders, to facilitate the development of resilience performance standards for infrastructure.

Hurricane Sandy Rebuilding Strategy: Stronger Communities, A Resilient Region.

conversations among different representatives. Reality tells us there is a clear need for a comprehensive approach, and after a day of real time practice, everyone wants to continue the conversations.

The workshop makes clear that getting all stakeholders together to think about the interrelationships between infrastructure, energy, water purification, ecology and so on brings real insight. The maps and analyses make clear that projects influence each other; the next question is what to do about that. One of the outcomes is that we begin to organize the task force regionally around the guidelines, so that the spending is more comprehensively organized—an approach partially inspired by my Dutch experience in regional infrastructure investments.

This collective insight about the need for ongoing collaboration is, of course, the one I was hoping for. Out of it, we develop the "Infrastructure Resilience Guidelines" as a task force recommendation for relief funding: investments in recovery should take a place-based, comprehensive approach. Funding agencies will be obliged to translate these principles into their work as they allocate money to the states and cities. If this recommendation sticks, it alone accomplishes real institutional change—change happening well below the radar, deep in the federal government, but I find it exciting because it challenges the existing power structure. If HUD and FEMA and DOT and the Corps sit down together and actually synchronize their plans, the role of the White House must change too. No longer the integrator at the end of the process, the team at 1600 Pennsylvania Avenue would have to steer integration from the start as part of the collaboration. For every agency, this would be a big step, a change in the way they define their turf and their conceptions of success. Rather than achieve the most themselves, they would seek to achieve the best results together with others. It's a very Dutch concept. Can it work in America? I am convinced it can.

Do You Really Think This Is the Right Way?

It is precisely this integration that is critical to shaping the competition. It's clear after the workshop that the problems, and thus the solutions, are deeply intertwined, so it's critical that every affected organization participate. The thrust of our effort has to be on integration. The task force science group, led by the National Oceanic and Atmospheric Administration (NOAA), is compiling a comprehensive resource package for the teams that will compete. NOAA, which embodies a culture of proceeding from learning to understanding to integration, is enthusiastic about the competition. They agree that this is the right approach for dealing comprehensively with complex challenges, and it's great to have them as a partner. Not everyone is convinced of our approach, and I need as many partners as possible in these critical early days. Rebuild by Design is still an abstraction, and for some a threat: unfamiliar, unreliable, unwieldy and vague. There are grantees who just want access to relief funds so they can do what they usually do; HUD staff who agree with them; White House staff who see a clear risk

NOAA

of failure and don't want failure on the president's plate; and individuals throughout the system who don't comprehend or appreciate the opportunity that we see.

Those doubters notwithstanding, in May, the task force convenes with Donovan to seek his formal approval of the Rebuild by Design project. He asks me to take him through it one more time, which I do: first there is a call for talent, an invitation to interdisciplinary teams from all over the world. To attract the broadest groups to work across the board on all the region's challenges, we divide the call into different categories: coastal, urban, ecological and a catch-all. After we select teams, there is a coordinated research stage. This focuses on vulnerabilities and interdependencies, enabling teams to identify opportunities to transform the region. Teams will develop their proposals and we will select the most promising ones, seeking projects in diverse places, politically supported and able to address the full scope of the challenges on the ground. In the final stage, teams will build coalitions with local stakeholders to design and develop these transformative projects together. The result we envision is ten inspirational, transformative designs that are eligible for Community Development Block Grant Disaster Recovery funding, ready to move toward implementation. We intend to avoid a top-down approach in which direction comes from us. The competition should be wide open, relying on discovery and collaboration.

Everything goes quiet as Donovan asks me, "Do you really think this is the right way?" I sense that he trusts me but is attuned to the skepticism of others. This, I feel, is the go or no-go moment. This is why I came to the U.S. "Yes!" I reply—a little too loudly. I am convinced that this is the best approach, desperately needed and the perfect opportunity. "Okay, then we'll do it!" Donovan says, and I hear the excitement and commitment in his voice. At that moment, I feel as if there is only one member of the entire task force team who shares my belief in Rebuild by Design, and that is Shaun Donovan. Even the supporters in the room have their doubts. Laurel Blatchford wants it to happen but sees her role as protecting Shaun from failure and isn't convinced this won't be one. Marion McFadden wants the process to be bold and transformative for vulnerable communities but doesn't fully grasp how the competition process will yield that. Josh Sawislak is a proponent of holistic planning but skeptical that the federal government can pull it off. Kevin Bush believes in the concept but has similar doubts about our ability to execute. Scott Davis hopes we can realize our ambitions for a truly comprehensive approach to rebuilding without anybody noticing.

But Shaun's commitment is the one that matters. And we have it.

After that meeting, Rebuild by Design is moved to the appendices of the draft task force report, the Hurricane Sandy Rebuilding Strategy. At this point all we have is a "go" from the task force chair—no funding, no budget. By shifting the project to the appendices, we take it out of the weekly spotlight. Here, I am promised, we can incubate and build momentum, seeking funding. Still, "in the appendix" sounds like it might be close to "kicked out the door." How can I get it upfront again and into the political spotlight?

Rebuild by Design's relegation to the appendices seems a setback, but I come to see it as an opportunity. Under the radar, it can mature and expand as we work on getting outside support and build on our outside partnerships. Then it will become an inevitability. I believe this because, despite all the skepticism, after the decisive meeting with Shaun none of the players steps back. No one says, "Count me out." Everyone keeps working on it, thinking about it, and helping out. The fuzzy and unfamiliar nature of what we are doing causes some agencies to want to hold Rebuild by Design at arm's length. But the opportunity it presents causes them to hang on, too. Here in the United States, opportunities are valued. There is a "what if" quality to the opportunity to innovate. Nobody knows yet how much money is at stake—a few hundred million, or billions?—and there's a general sense that Rebuild by Design may misfire. But there's also a "let's give it a try" sentiment. Behind the scenes, in countless conversations, Donovan and task force leaders Laurel Blatchford and Marion McFadden keep pushing.

Although Donovan heads up the Department of Housing and Urban Design, his is not the only approval we need. We must also convince the White House Office of Management and Budget (OMB), which controls CDBG-DR funding. They are skeptical. This is what I hear: "You want an open process, Henk? A coalition of everyone, but you won't say exactly what it will achieve? Because you need the coordinated research first to decide what is needed most? And where? And then you want to work with everyone on designing solutions? So not only with the government, but the private sector and the communities? With all this uncertainty, you are asking the federal government to commit as much as a billion dollars for projects whose chances of success are not necessarily guaranteed, as your whole approach is about innovation? In other words, you want the president to sign off on Rebuild by Design without knowing the scope, the definition of success, or the expected outcome? You are asking for a presidential commitment to a double risk of failure."

Yes. That is all true. Rebuild by Design is about ambition and inclusion. It is a comprehensive, innovative approach without any guarantees of successfully impacting the communities affected by Sandy. I am asking the federal government to dare to change, because change promises greater effectiveness. It comes with the risk of failure, so I am not surprised that this is a hard pill for people in power to swallow. I am banking that President Obama, who has tried to navigate his administration toward change and innovation in many areas, will understand and embrace our approach. I make it clear to OMB that we don't need a funding commitment—not yet. What we need now is agreement to partner and to proceed, with the federal government in the lead and with the understanding that if we produce transformative projects they will be funded. My ideas are not crazy, and they can only be evaluated if we begin. I am asking OMB to bless an approach built on opportunity-based decision-making, not risk-averse management.

Donovan's leadership in this moment is crucial. He intends to use part of the relief budget to fund innovative

↓ Long Beach, New York, a week after the storm

Shaun Donovan
Interview p.46

"A really important part of leadership is making sure that people who work for you know that when they're taking risks, if something goes wrong, which it inevitably will when you're trying something new, that I will have their backs and say that was my decision, not their fault. As long as you're taking risks for the right reason, if you're not failing, you're not taking enough risk."

outcomes and to seek partnerships and funding to leverage federal resources. He is intent on demonstrating that the way we prepare for disasters can be different and better, and he campaigns behind the scenes for this approach. But he is savvy enough to leave himself room to maneuver. He won't commit any funds yet. When asked how much money Rebuild by Design may involve, he replies, "Possibly billions." People hear what they want in that answer, since it could just as easily mean nothing at all. Instead of committing too early, he uses this ambiguity to ask others to join, telling them "I'll do my utmost best, but I expect from you that we manage that success together." This is how he uses his role as task force chair to lead in both the public and private arenas that intersect in the recovery effort.

His approach instills confidence in his legal team, his policy makers, the larger task force, the White House—and me. He asks me to make Rebuild by Design as smart as possible, and he tells a reporter, tongue in cheek, "We just do whatever Henk tells us." It's a joke, but Donovan knows what he's doing. That public endorsement puts me in a position to act. Now no one asks whether or not I am speaking on behalf of the Secretary. Internally, we debate and disagree, of course, but publicly Donovan has the back of everyone on the task force, who in turn are willing to go the extra mile for him.

TOO BIG
to Simplify

Embrace Complexity

Embrace Complexity

Climate change connects to changing demographics, urbanization, economy and ecology. The risks posed by floods are intertwined with basic needs for clean water, food, energy and prosperity. These risks and needs show clear and strong interdependencies on a regional, often metropolitan scale—the scale where mankind can act to adapt to and mitigate climate risks. It is here, in this complexity of interdependencies, that we find opportunities. With everything interlinked, a comprehensive approach always yields multiple benefits. The need to protect ourselves and our systems can support a desire to improve our environment, too. Investments in ecological system may well strengthen the economy. The places where this complexity converges are the hotspots of today and tomorrow, where the opportunity for change is greatest. Here, we can make the switch from risk to reward and add value in multiple ways.

Embrace Complexity

To make this switch, we must take the time to truly understand how things work. That requires discipline, for in the face of a crisis, slowing down to understand can seem like unnecessary hesitation. But we can only make good plans when we know what is at stake, know how our environmental, societal and economic systems interconnect, and thoroughly understand the real vulnerabilities in our cities, regions and nations. That means looking for the right questions instead of quick answers to isolated problems. It means comprehending regional and local conditions, interests and expectations and how these interact with larger scale systems. It is only through that deep understanding that we discover the actual opportunities for change.

Embrace Complexity

Deep understanding doesn't come from an outsider's professional perspective, nor from data models alone. We must collaborate with the people who live and work in these hotspots of complexity to understand what is happening and what is at stake. This requires inclusive research, bringing together not only specialists and academics but entrepreneurs, decision-makers, activists and local officials. Shared ownership of the questions evolves into shared ownership of the answers, so that complex problems are met with sustainable interventions that solve real problems for everyone.

The most controversial and threatening aspect of what we are proposing is how funds will be delivered to the states and cities. The Sandy relief funding HUD manages takes the form of Community Development Block Grant Disaster Recovery funds. In a business–as–usual scenario, those funds would be allocated according to a distribution formula based on the amount of damage caused by a disaster. The states and cities affected—the grantees—draw up plans for how to spend the money in accordance with HUD's guidelines, and HUD hands over the funds. In this arrangement, the federal government exerts limited control over how the money is spent. Grantees refer to the federal funding as a right—"our money," they call it—distributed to them by Congress, which after all, is supposed to represent them.

Rebuild by Design intends to challenge this relationship, inserting the federal government much more aggressively into determining how funds are spent. It is an assault upon, or at least a sharp poke at, the very heart of the federal political

"How often in government do you get the chance to innovate? The stars were really aligned. It was a region that I knew very well and cared about. We just had the re-election of President Obama, and he was beginning his second term. Shaun Donovan and I had been in the administration for a long time and built up relationships, without which we never could have done the complicated inter-agency work. FEMA was really willing to put money into recovery in a different way, not just response. So there was a desire to get things done differently than in other disasters, to show that the federal government could be responsive and effective. There was a real set of needs on the ground, money that had to be spent. All of those things in different contexts constitute urgency. You need to move different agendas through government than would otherwise go. So we had an Executive Order of the President, we had a requirement to collaborate and innovate and the ability–the social capital–to do that. And we had a deadline, and I'm really a big fan of deadlines. We had a 180-day frame to lay the foundation

Laurel Blatchford

Chief of Staff of the U.S. Department of Housing and Urban Development (HUD) from 2009 to 2013 and Executive Director of the Hurricane Sandy Rebuilding Task Force from January to September 2013

for all the work that came out of the task force, including Rebuild by Design. My goal was to create the biggest, best, most forward-looking mandate for all these things that had to be done on the longer term. We were laying the tracks for those longer-term projects. Because we all knew that it wasn't going to be a 180-day process to rebuild that region. So the Executive Order empowered us to focus on the longer term in a very meaningful, time-bounded way, with the resources to produce the report and its recommendations. It allowed us to have a conversation about the longer term while dealing with the shorter term. It allowed us to connect it to the funding that was being appropriated, and then it set up the longer-term work itself, because you couldn't do Rebuild by Design in 180 days either; we had to create a timeline that worked for both."

system. States and cities will not be the sole arbiters of how relief funds are spent on projects that arise out of the Rebuild by Design process. Those grantees are part of the task force's Advisory Group, and we want them to commit to sharing their power. We want them to join with the federal government and other, nongovernmental stakeholders to collectively agree on what will be built—and then to go build it.

We definitely need their commitment—but not yet. Because Rebuild by Design was moved to the appendix of the draft task force report, we are less visible amid the commotion of the recovery. There is an enormous amount of work being done in New York and New Jersey, and Rebuild by Design—nicknamed "Vague by Design" inside the task force—represents a small piece of the effort. The recovery offices of New York, New Jersey and New York City, led by their respective "Sandy czars," may wonder what we are up

Marc Ferzan
Interview p.158

"Remember, at the time we were coming out of the disaster, tremendous need had been identified, there was widespread devastation throughout the state, and a design competition was announced with the caveat that not everyone was going to win. That creates tension for public messaging for many reasons."

to. But they are busy, and the dynamics of the many initiatives underway create space for us to maneuver, innovate and quietly build support.

We are also able to take advantage of the urgency of the situation and the pressure to move ahead, to get things done. We are able to push through impediments that could have doomed the project in a normal situation. For example, Rebuild by Design is supposed to comply with the Paperwork Reduction Act, a federal law aimed at reducing bureaucratic burden on the public but implemented through a very bureaucratic system within the government. Compliance involves following a rigid process that our attorneys tell us will take six months. We barely have six months to finish our work! So calmly, openly, we ignore them. From now on, we are violators of the Paperwork Reduction Act. It is a badge of honor.

President Obama's Climate Action Plan

In the summer of 2009, Barack Obama proposed legislation to drastically reduce CO_2 emissions, but the Senate blocked it. Four years later and three months after Hurricane Sandy devastated the Northeast, Obama prioritized climate change in his second term as President. "We, the people, still believe that our obligations as Americans are not just to ourselves, but to all posterity," he said in his second inaugural address to Congress. "We will respond to the threat of climate change, knowing that the failure to do so would betray our children and future generations. Some may still deny the overwhelming judgment of science, but none can avoid the devastating impact of raging fires and crippling drought and more powerful storms."

Obama's policy was to both mitigate climate change and adapt to it. The President's Council on Environmental Quality (CEQ) worked on a Climate Action Plan to reduce climate change, while the Sandy Task Force worked on ways to adapt to it. When the White House releases the Climate Action Plan in June, Rebuild by Design has been adopted into it. Under the heading "Building Stronger and Safer Communities and Infrastructure," the plan declares, "In August 2013, President Obama's Hurricane Sandy Rebuilding Task Force will deliver

CEQ

APR 29, 2013.   CENTER FOR AMERICAN PROGRESS

Disastrous Spending:
Federal Disaster-Relief Expenditures Rise amid More Extreme Weather

"Sandy was the worst natural disaster in the United States in terms of destruction and deaths since Hurricanes Katrina and Rita in 2005, but it wasn't the only one. In 2011 and 2012 alone, the United States experienced 25 floods, storms, droughts, heat waves, and wildfires that each caused at least $1 billion in damages. Combined, these extreme weather events were responsible for 1,107 fatalities and up to $188 billion in economic damages. The Center for American Progress conducted an analysis and found that the federal government—which means taxpayers—spent $136 billion total from fiscal year 2011 to fiscal year 2013 on disaster relief. This adds up to an average of nearly $400 per household per year.

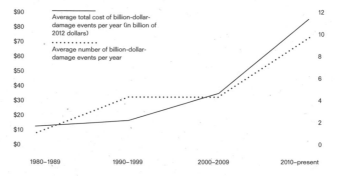

Billions of dollars in damages from extreme weather events increasing in frequency, cost from 1980-2012.
Source: National Oceanic and Atmospheric Administration

Data from the past 60 years reveals an increase in both presidential disaster declarations and extreme weather events that cause $1 billion or more in damages. If this trend continues at the same rate, the United States will experience more frequent and severe extreme weather events in the years to come, meaning that the federal government will have to spend more and more funds on disaster-relief efforts, leaving tax-payers with the bill."

to the President a rebuilding strategy to be implemented in Sandy-affected regions and establishing precedents that can be followed elsewhere. The task force and federal agencies are also piloting new ways to support resilience in the Sandy-affected region; the task force, for example, is hosting a regional 'Rebuilding by Design' competition to generate innovative solutions to enhance resilience." No longer are we relegated to an appendix; the president's public endorsement means Rebuild by Design is a reality even before it has been launched. Now things are moving. Yet we still don't know how we are going to actually start.

The money to stage the Rebuild by Design competition cannot come from the federal government. So where will we find it? In the United States, questions like this are answered by philanthropic organizations that often work closely with governments. The Department of Housing and Urban Development even has an Office for International Philanthropic Innovation (IPI). With my IPI colleagues Stewart Sarkozy-Banoczy and Justin Scheid, I meet with a group of potential donors and sponsors, including The Rockefeller Foundation, The Clinton Global Initiative and many others, big and small, regional and global. We meet in the Federal Building in downtown Manhattan, where all the federal agencies have their offices. Some thirty people are present, representing most of the major philanthropic organizations in the New York-New Jersey region. I have two hours to sell them on Rebuild by Design as a worthy investment.

My approach and objectives are straightforward. I am not making an ask today. I simply want some of these representatives to become interested enough in what we're doing to keep talking to us. So I present the process and the expected impact of Rebuild by Design, and then answer their questions. They are eager to understand, and not just out of curiosity. Each organization has its own mandates and objectives, and their questions reflect their interests. Does Rebuild by Design sufficiently address the vulnerable communities in the region? Are we really going to do something with that thing called "resilience"? Is there enough focus on the City of New York? Aren't we forgetting the coastal communities? Is New Jersey really involved? Are we going to protect the business district? Are the architects in a sufficiently strong position to realize innovative designs? Are we going to improve the federal government's approach to climate change as well?

I realize that these foundations will not fund our plan because I think it is good. If they fund us at all, they will do so only because

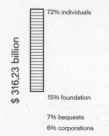

Charitable donations in the U.S. in 2013.

Based on: Giving USA: The annual report on philanthropy for the year 2013.

83

Rebuild by Design aligns with their own goals and objectives. In subsequent days, I have follow-up talks with ten organizations. I knew when I raised my hand and told Shaun Donovan I wanted to help that I would have to take on many challenges, but I had not imagined I would end up working as a fundraiser, pitching resilience, sustainability, design, innovation and rebuilding to philanthropic gatekeepers. I am a salesman for Rebuild by Design, learning about their goals and ambitions, showing how the design competition could support them, always answering the implicit question of what's in it for them. The lack of certainty around Rebuild by Design is problematic. How much money, they wonder, are we talking about? Shaun Donovan has said "up to a billion dollars," but that's pretty imprecise. The federal distribution formula is likely to split funding roughly into thirds for New York City, New York state and New Jersey, so there's some guidance, and the CDBG-DR funds are focused on vulnerable communities, so there's a little more. But I have no guarantees. As I have with everyone else so far, I ask the foundation representatives with whom I meet to join us on the faith, at least in part, that together we can find the best opportunities for meaningful change.

I have a lot of meetings, but I don't receive a lot of checks. In fact, I don't receive any checks. The design competition is supposed to launch publicly on June 20, and with a week to go, I have zero funding for it. Are we going to have to cancel? It's unthinkable. After all, the president of the United States is expecting us to pull this off. We need four million dollars so we can spend a billion, and although I have had many promising conversations, I do not have the money in hand.

And then we get a break. On June 13, Shaun Donovan is to host a gala of the Municipal Arts Society at Grand Central Station, where he will present the Jacqueline Kennedy Onassis Medal to Dr. Judith Rodin, president of The Rockefeller Foundation. My conversations with Nancy Kete of The Rockefeller Foundation have been promising, and I harbor the hope that they may become our biggest sponsor. I arrive in Grand Central Station early when, through what seems to be an extraordinary bit of serendipity, I encounter Rodin herself in the glorious Grand Hall of the station. I seize my opportunity.

She tells me she is a fan of the Netherlands, once met our then Queen Beatrix, and is aware of the tremendous efforts by our Prince (now King) Willem Alexander on behalf of global water management. She has inspiring stories to tell about her Dutch adventures and about water. Soon, the conversation turns to Sandy, the risks for the region, climate change, the need to improve fast and the opportunities Rebuild by Design might offer. Donovan finds his moment with her later in the evening and lends his support to Rebuild by Design. Later, Rodin and I speak again, and she tells me what I have been aching to hear: The Rockefeller Foundation will donate more than half of what we need to stage the competition.

"We believe that partnership is the new form of leadership in the 21st century. That nobody has the resources and nobody has all of the knowledge, or frankly the capacity, to go it alone."

Judith Rodin
Interview p.90

I am filled with relief. It is enough to start, and with Rockefeller on board, I know that we will be able to bring other funders in to fill the gap. Rodin and Rockefeller's endorsement is a massively important signal to everyone who has been watching us: Rebuild by Design is for real. We will benefit not only from their money and their endorsement but also their regional base and their support groups. If I learned anything during my weeks of soliciting foundations, it was that our objectives would have to mesh with those of our funders. Now, conversely, I know that we will need to find funders from throughout our region, for the foundations' interests would inevitably shape our work. It will not be tenable to arrive in New Jersey supported only by New York-based foundations.

Back in D.C., I come to a fuller appreciation of the significance of support from The Rockefeller Foundation. Such a prominent non-government partner possesses status in the political world. With Rockefeller on board, not only does the range of our supporters increase, but the validity of our vision takes a huge leap forward, as well. The credibility of Judith Rodin and The Rockefeller Foundation confers legitimacy we could not achieve on our own. Their commitment is inspirational and convincing at all levels of that government.

A Strong Coalition

At the root of Rebuild by Design is our intention that this must be more than a competition that produces winners. It must be truly inclusive, and use that inclusivity to collectively discover the region's resilience needs. This requires a strong coalition, and I discover a key partner in Eric Klinenberg, professor of sociology and director of the Institute of Public Knowledge (IPK) at New York University. Although it is an academic institution, IPK under Eric takes a quasi–activist approach to its work. Eric and I connect right away; he understands Rebuild by Design better than anyone I have met besides Shaun. He immediately grasps why the collective nature of Rebuild by Design's process is so important, and as head of IPK, he understands how to make it work. So does Sam Carter, Eric's associate director, who agrees to manage the research process. I leave buoyed by the knowledge that I have found kindred spirits.

My discussions with Eric and Sam reinforce my growing belief that the research and design stages of Rebuild by Design should have separate formats and separate partnerships. The research stage must focus on understanding the region, its systems, processes, people, culture and conditions. From this, we can conduct an analysis that identifies opportunities for smart interventions. Organizations like IPK fit in here. The design stage will depend upon coalitions of stakeholders collectively seeking solutions, and that will require a different kind of supporting partner.

IPK

Eric Klinenberg
Interview p.96

"I knew that if we were going to make investments in climate security, there was a risk that we would wind up protecting the most connected people and places, the communities that have the most political capital and ability to get resources directed towards themselves. I wanted to make sure that in our process the most vulnerable people and places would get priority."

In my search, I meet with Rob Pirani and Rob Lane from the Regional Plan Association (RPA), Mary Row from the Municipal Arts Society (MAS), and David van der Leer from the Van Alen Institute (VAI). As with all nonprofits, each brings a distinct set of perspectives and assets to the table. The Regional Plan Association excels at regional planning and policy making. Municipal Arts Society is embedded in New York's culture of public arts. And the Van Alen Institute is experienced in architectural design competitions focusing on community design. The truth is I don't need any one of these as partners, I need all of them. I convene a meeting with all three together, and am surprised to discover that Rob, Mary and David do not know one another yet. This is an opportunity in itself; Rebuild by Design can be a chance for them to work together and find their own synergies. One thing is certain: if the three of them work together then I will have the coalition I need to facilitate the design process, just as the Institute of Public Knowledge will lead the research process. Slowly, the puzzle is coming together.

No Turning Back

At four o'clock on the morning of June 20, Kevin Bush and I finish preparations for that day's launch announcement. We have completed the Design Brief, the Request for Qualifications, the formal announcement of the design competition—everything the bureaucracy demands. A few hours later, Shaun stands before hundreds of people in the hall at NYU's Institute for Public Knowledge and formally opens the competition.

Looking around the room, I see many faces I now know well, five months after I volunteered to create this thing that has taken on a life of its own. Judith Rodin is on stage with Shaun and me, as The Rockefeller Foundation is our primary philantropic partner. So is IPK Director Eric Klinenberg, our host and research stage partner. Perhaps the most significant guests, though, are Mark Ferzan, Seth Diamond and Seth Pinsky. They are the Sandy czars, respectively, of New Jersey, New York and New York City. By their presence, they publicly connect the design process to the grantees who must ultimately build what Rebuild by Design produces. Indeed, by virtue of their presence, everyone in the room is validating what we have done. They see each other, they know this is real. The media present see them too, and I am grateful for their presence. Now, we have to attract the world's top talent, and that means getting the word out to the world.

With the project launched, I turn my attention to finding the balance of the four million–plus dollars we need to see it through. While Rockefeller's endorsement and their millions have been critical to our success, they have also complicated things. I had thought that other funders would fall in line quickly once Rockefeller made the first move, but the opposite has happened. With Rockefeller as the lead supporter, smaller foundations now worry that their interests would be overshadowed. I argue that, to the contrary, Rebuild by Design offers them an opportunity to multiply their effectiveness through collaboration. The conversations are long and detailed, but one by one, five additional foundations come on board. In addition to The Rockefeller Foundation we are supported by the JPB Foundation, Hearst Foundation, Deutsche Bank New York Foundation, Surdna Foundation and New Jersey Recovery

Shaun Donovan launches Rebuild by Design.

Fund. Our coalition grows in terms of funding but also interests and ambitions. This demonstration of breadth and strength is exactly what I am looking for.

I raise enough money to run the support process for eight teams. Can we get another $400,000—enough to fund the ten we envision? Shaun and I start to turn the screws on our donors. We schedule a call with Barbara Pickower, president of the JPB Foundation. I am waiting for Shaun, who is late to start the call, when my cell phone rings. It's Dana Bourland, JPB's sustainability director: "We will donate the extra $400,000 to get you to the needed ten teams!"

Fantastic! We have our millions. Now we can figure out how to spend our billion.

DR. JUDITH RODIN–"We need to think differently and we need to build processes and expertise around that more integrated way of thinking. <u>It's central to the future of the planet.</u> It's about how you really approach the 21st century and think about the capacity to be nimble, the capacity to fail safely, the capacity to be more aware and to be able to make change in real time."

Dr. Judith Rodin

President of The Rockefeller Foundation from 2005 to 2017 and author of The Resilience Dividend: Being Strong in a World Where Things Go Wrong.

JELTE BOEIJENGA   Where did Rebuild by Design start for you?

JUDITH RODIN   After Superstorm Sandy hit, Andrew Cuomo, the governor of New York, appointed a commission on the recovery and I co-chaired it. The Rockefeller Foundation staffed it and paid for the consultants and we brought together experts around the areas that needed to focus on recovery: energy, transportation, land-use, financing and the like. And the reason that I saw it as an opportunity and agreed to chair it–other than civic mindedness–was that we felt that if the rebuilding process could be done through a resilience building lens in an iconic city like New York, then it could have global transformational capacity. And New York would be better prepared for whatever hit next. We saw all kinds of striking things in our initial analysis. The reason so many generators flooded, for example, is because after New York was hit from the air on 9/11, many of the businesses put their backup generator in the basement. So we wanted to really infuse the narrative that you can't always predict what the next crisis is going to be. And that these resilience building principles don't require a crystal ball. They require building-in the capacity to be more aware, to be nimble, to be able to adjust more flexibly, to have multiple uses for each expense.

And during that time, Shaun Donovan was appointed head of the federal Sandy Task Force and as this recovery process unfolded, Shaun and I worked closely together, Shaun as the chair of the federal response, and I as the co-chair of the New York State response. So once these reports were complete, using this resilience narrative, we asked ourselves whether we could do something really creative and different with a billion dollars of federal funds. And we started talking about Rebuild by Design. It seemed like a natural fit. When Sandy hit, Rockefeller had already funded the Asian Cities Climate Change Resilience Network, working primarily with cities that were on river deltas or coasts in vulnerable Asian countries. And after Hurricane Katrina we invested in pulling together the players who created the rebuilding framework for the city of New Orleans, working with local and state and federal officials, as well as local philanthropies and others. So it was consistent with work we'd already done in recoveries after catastrophic emergencies. And it was also consistent with our strategy that it was really about what that rebuilding could do, not only for that region, but also for shaping a broader narrative about the importance of building resilience in advance, rather than only during times of recovery. So we were into it in a big way and it was a perfect match. And Shaun knew that.

"You can't always predict what the next crisis is going to be."

91

JB Why would The Rockefeller Foundation invest money in a process of which you could also argue that it is primarily the responsibility of government, be it federal, state or local? What does The Rockefeller Foundation want to achieve with this?

"We want to transform systems and identify big incredible needs, where we think we might have a unique role to play with partners."

JR It's important to say that The Rockefeller Foundation is America's first global philanthropy and for the first maybe 30 or 40 years of its existence, it was giving more foreign aid than the U.S. government. So it has a history and DNA essentially that says: it doesn't matter what sector we come from, we want to transform systems and identify big incredible needs, where we think we might have a unique role to play with partners. And when I started as the foundation's president, it was very clear to me that if we only used dollars to give grants, we were not getting sufficient leverage and we're not engaging in the strategic partnerships that really allow for transformational impact. And those partnerships often are about what the bilateral donors are doing. The Netherlands, the Norwegians, the British, USAID and others, became very significant strategic partners of ours in our global work. So it

was only natural that state, city and the U.S. government would be natural partners when it was domestic work. But actually, we didn't spend a lot of money on this. What we did was fund what the federal government couldn't fund. So when Shaun said: I have a billion dollars to spend, but I don't have the five million to run the competition, it seemed perfect. We could really be partners. Often people think of partnering as you all putting the same amount of money into a pot and it does one thing. We see partnering as each entity having the capacity to actually do what it does best, and then leverage one another and really do something that neither one could do alone.

We believe that partnership is the new form of leadership in the 21st century. That nobody has the resources and nobody has all of the knowledge, or frankly the capacity, to go it alone. Even governments. So we often collaborate with governments. And sometimes they are funding-partners and sometimes they are grantees. We just made a multi-million dollar grant to the Kenyan government for the digital jobs training program for unemployed Kenyan youth, as part of an initiative to transform job opportunities in Africa more broadly. And there the best actor with the broadest training capacity is often the government itself. So they're our grantee. Other times we'll partner with the government, as we did in Rebuild by Design, where we each put in different kinds of resources. Strategic partners where your strategies are aligned—how you engage in the process, who you include—are critical to the outcome. But that takes discussion in the beginning, so that you're really sure that your strategies aren't going to bump up against each other at some point. So we spent a lot of time and energy on building that trust on the front end.

(JB) You mentioned transformational impact. Transformation of what? And in what direction?

(JR) We're always looking at the end point for people, the beneficiaries, to have their lives improved by the outcome. That is our mission. And for us, it means transforming systems that improve the lives of people, that make social impact, have economic impact or protective impact. Particularly of the poor and vulnerable who often are in the most impacted places when emergencies hit, whether they're climate-related or man-made. So consistent with that mission, we are looking for systems transformation that protects and improves the lives of people. And we saw this as one of them, because part of the goal here was not only to rebuild but to get multiple benefits from each investment. Whether it's government making the investment or private sector or philanthropy, to get a single outcome for a single investment is not something we ought to be accepting in the 21st century. Nobody has enough money to do that. We can no longer afford to

spend money in silos. We should really construct our thinking in ways that we can get multiple wins for each dollar.

So we need to think differently and we need to build processes and expertise around that more integrated way of thinking. To facilitate this, a resilience framework is critical. Because it's not only about infrastructure or rebuilding. It's central to the future of the planet, I think. It's about how you really approach the 21st century and think about the capacity to be nimble, the capacity to fail safely, the capacity to be more aware and to be able to make change in real time. All of those things that we saw fail in Sandy, in Katrina and in so many other places. And Rebuild by Design infused that thinking into the process. Each of the projects that won, provides multiple benefits for the rebuild investment and all of them benefit people and communities as the recipients. That's what we call the resilience dividend. And both design thinking and systems thinking allow you to think this way. It's not design, it's design thinking. Architecture is design, but not every architect engages in design thinking. And you don't need to be an architect to engage in design thinking.

> "We are looking for systems transformation that protects and improves the lives of people."

JB   Has Rebuild by Design influenced other work by The Rockefeller Foundation?

(JR)   After Rebuild by Design was successful we took it to the national level in the United States, with the National Disaster Resilience Competition. Again, we funded two things: a competition–HUD had an additional billion dollars–but we also then developed a curriculum, called Resilience Academies. All counties or cities that had had a federally declared disaster in the prior two years were eligible to apply, but they couldn't compete unless they attended one of the Resilience Academies. And that was a first for the United States government. And looking at the outcome, it's very clear that we not only transformed the way the affected communities fundamentally thought about what the vulnerabilities were that made a disruption become a disaster, but also that they needed to rebuild therefore in a completely different way. We also used Resilience Academies to train the people in the federal agencies who were going to be the judges in the competition. And we had a dual reason for doing that. Obviously, we wanted to make them better judges, but we wanted it to impact going forward, how they would spend other money. If you're in the Department of Transportation and suddenly you're trained in resilience thinking and design thinking, you're going to look at transportation projects differently. And the same with FEMA and with HUD. So again, for us, there was the opportunity to make a relatively small financial investment but contribute a tremendous investment of expertise.

And the other thing for us is that by then we had launched 100 Resilient Cities, that began in 2013. And part of what we did in Rebuild by Design, we are replicating in 100 cities around the world. What's fascinating is we had 1100 cities apply, from all six continents. And to really understand, from the applications, their experience of the shocks and slower-burning stresses that they were being exposed to in infrastructure, climate change, and social unrest, in economic decline. And again, bringing a system's transformation, resilience thinking and design thinking together in the 100 cities that did win the competition, has been extraordinary.

"We can no longer afford to spend money in silos. We should really construct our thinking in ways that we can get multiple wins for each dollar."

With ARUP, the global engineering and design company, we have built a City Resilience Index. It diagnoses the whole system of the city. From the thinking developed in Rebuild by Design it analyzes social, economic, as well as natural and built infrastructure, but also governance. Because one of the things that was clear in the Rebuild by Design work was that the governance, the structure of the building and rebuilding process, who gets to have a say about what, is a very important part in the success of the outcomes. What we learned in New Orleans, what failed, is that experts got parachuted in very quickly and they had great architectural or engineering ideas, but the communities felt both excluded and unheard. And they had ideas too; they were the ones who were going to live there. They really understand the nuances of the environment and the context. The great ideas don't only come when a group of experts sits around at a conference table and thinks them up.

> "What we learned in New Orleans, is that experts got parachuted in very quickly, but the communities felt both excluded and unheard."

We learned from that experience how important community participation was. So that was a central part of Rebuild by Design, which was really quite unique and actually quite difficult. But we watched how different the outcomes became when we integrated the experts and the diverse sectors of experts with communities who have local knowledge. So we have now built, into the strategies of all of our 100 cities, deep involvement by the local communities, civil society, academics, the private sector. Of those 1100 cities that applied, no city won if they weren't really able to identify how they were engaging all of these sectors. They didn't have to have the answers yet in terms of their strategies to build resilience, but they had to have the right constituents to build the answers and realize the resilience dividend.

▲

ERIC KLINENBERG–"Any design should do more than simply protect a place from extreme weather or another shock, it should also improve the quality of life every day. That requires an approach which is not just about designing engineering systems or structures, but also about how people will use them, be affected by them and how people will reshape the structures as they come together."

Eric Klinenberg

Research director of Rebuild by Design
and Director of the Institute of Public Knowledge, New York University.

JELTE BOEIJENGA   What, as a researcher and director of the Institute of Public Knowledge, attracted you to the idea of Rebuild by Design?

ERIC KLINENBERG   First, I was surprised by the decision to ask a social scientist to be the research director of a design competition. The more conventional choice would have been to go to an architect or an urban planner. But the fact that they asked a social scientist with a track record of doing research on issues like inequality in extreme events, meant that they were interested in a different kind of process. So for a time it was just hard to believe. And then, when I realized it was real, and there was a serious possibility of doing research that could actually lead to a stronger and more resilient and climate aware region, we got very excited. From the time that Sandy hit, we had started to work on what had happened. I had a history of doing research on these issues before, and I had just taken over this institute, and publicly announced that it was going to focus on climate change and the future of cities, with a focus on this city in particular. So we were already working very hard on the problem and we realized this could be an opportunity to do something really different. The only question for me was how to gracefully exit from other projects and throw ourselves into this.

JB   Did you have a specific agenda with Rebuild by Design?

EK   There were a few principles that I wanted to integrate into the program, as a social scientist. Because of my particular research, we had an interest in social infrastructure and what happens to these designs when they hit the streets, which I think most people don't focus on quite as much. So one principle was that any design that came out of the competition should do more than simply protect a place from extreme weather or another shock. Design should not just be about disaster planning, it should also improve the quality of life every day. I wanted every design idea to have multiple benefits. And that would require an approach which is not just about designing engineering systems or structures, but also about how people will use them, be affected by structures and how people will reshape the structures as they come together. That is really what we had not done after September 11, for instance, when we redesigned New York City and many other critical infrastructures to be more secure against a terrorist attack.

"The process of building homeland security made everything a little bit worse: our cities became uglier, our systems became less efficient and less pleasant. And I knew that climate security had to work differently."

But we didn't make the cities and the systems that we rely on every day any better in the process. In fact, the process of building homeland security made everything a little bit worse: our cities became uglier, our systems became less efficient and less pleasant. And I knew that climate security had to work differently.

> **"If you want to protect people and get the most use of your resources, you should focus on people and places who need help most."**

Secondly, I knew that if we were going to make investments in climate security, there was a risk that we would wind up protecting the most connected people and places, the communities that have the most political capital and ability to get resources directed towards themselves. I wanted to make sure that in our process the most vulnerable people and places would get priority. So it was very important to me that issues of equity be on the table and that we wouldn't create a design competition that took care of institutions or places that actually already had good access to resources but neglected places that needed this kind of improvement as a matter of life and death.

JB   Is this a political stance or a notion derived from your research?

EK   I don't think of it as a political stance as much as a stance born of social science research. We know already which people and places are most vulnerable to the climate. We know, as a matter of record, that people and places that are vulnerable already, for a range of reasons, will be more susceptible to dangerous weather. They have fewer resources to protect themselves. So it's not a political matter as much as a scientific one, to say that if you want to protect people and get the most use of your resources, you should focus on people and places who need help most. But often that doesn't happen in politics. Often major resources go to communities that already have the most. The other thing that I tried to emphasize is that we wanted the design teams to have as rich an ethnographic understanding of how people lived in the places where they were considering design projects as they could have. There's a history of designers—especially in big competitions with a lot of money behind them—coming in and building projects from the top down, without carefully considering what people who live in those places want and need, or what they know already. And so, as a research director with experience in doing ethnographic research that involves community engagement, I pushed the teams to work hard on immersing themselves, getting to know people they might not know otherwise.

JB   Was Rebuild by Design—in a way—for you also an opportunity to see how the lessons from your research could be applied in practice?

EK   Very much so, that was very exciting for me. I worked very hard to push teams to consider the social infrastructure as a critical infrastructure. So that they weren't just building hard-lined systems to do flood prevention, so they would also think about how the designs they built would shape the way people interact. These were insights from social science that I thought could be very useful for this process. Of course, as a research director, I couldn't dictate what the groups did, but I could establish important issues for them to consider. And I could orient them towards certain kinds of problems that they might not otherwise consider. And many of the teams followed our advice; we saw many multi-purpose designs, we saw many proposals that were concerned with inequality, we really saw sociologically informed design ideas for the climate. So it was a reciprocally rewarding process, a virtuous circle. I was able to open up some avenues to explore and then the design teams discovered lots of things that I hadn't seen there. So I feel a personal connection to the projects that is very rewarding.

"The design competition worked in a dramatically different way than almost all others I know about."

I'm now writing a book about social infrastructure that includes a lot of ideas that I became aware of during the Rebuild by Design process. For instance the project in Hunts Point. The project is about how to protect one critical infrastructure, the food market that provides food for tens of millions of people in the region. But the PennDesign/OLIN team was able to integrate into that concerns about social infrastructure that I hadn't understood before. Everything from the physical surround of the market, the way in which it limits the mobility of people who live in the Hunts Point neighborhood to the way that it polluted the air and affected their health. So the design ultimately had both a component that involved flood management and a social infrastructure plan that would begin to address some of these very difficult problems. And in such a way that it helped local economic development and helped employment. And I hadn't seen all those possibilities before, before I saw the design team do its work. On Staten Island, the SCAPE team built up a social infrastructure complex that includes educational hubs. They built in these cultural resources that would provide young people and families throughout the city with a chance to learn more about our relationship with the water. So that's another area where the design teams recognized an opening and took it to a place that most people I know couldn't see. So I ended up learning a lot about possibilities for productive development that I hadn't seen before.

JB   What were the crucial ingredients for the process to be successful?

EK   As you know, there's still a lot of work to do. The projects have not broken ground and many things can happen before they're developed. So it's hard to claim that it's a success because we haven't seen anything yet, but so far it seems very exciting. There are a few things. The first is that the teams did not have specifically informed design ideas before the process began. It wasn't a competition that said: thank you for entering, please give us your best design. It was a competition that said: we're going to make you do all these things, before you can get to what would be the entry. So the research phase was genuinely a time for them to consider a whole variety of projects and places for intervention. And that simple fact meant that the design competition worked in a dramatically different way than almost all others I know about. And it made the research stage crucially important and that meant that the work we did had real significance. And I didn't do this alone. We assembled a network of experts each of whom had a different specialization, and collectively we helped to orient the teams on everything from climate science to social science to planning and law. We had engineers, we had climate scientists, lawyers, public health people, and I think that allowed us to tackle a pretty wide range of issues.

"Climate change is the kind of problem and challenge that requires that collaboration. And therefore changes the normal way we work."

The other thing is that in the research stage, somehow, we persuaded the competitors in Rebuild by Design to collaborate with each other. So instead of working against one another, they helped each other out. And climate change is the kind of problem and challenge that requires that collaboration. And therefore changes the normal way we work. And, we were fortunate to have very high-quality people. It was a remarkably open-minded group. I think Sandy made it clear that the way we were building things was wrong. It was no longer going to work. There was an urgent need to design things differently. We all wanted a different outcome and that meant that we were all open to a different process.

▲

ERIC KLINENBERG—"Sandy made it clear that the way we were building things was wrong. It was no longer going to work. There was an urgent need to design things differently. We all wanted a different outcome and that meant that we were all open to a different process."

KLAUS JACOB–"I'm not against what happens right now, but if that's the only thing that happens, we're doing future generations a disservice. These protective measures are important transition band-aids but if you rely just on band-aids without having a vision of what else is needed, it becomes a moral, ethical issue of intergenerational inequity and injustice."

Klaus Jacob

Member of the Research Advisory Group of Rebuild by Design and Special Research Scientist at the Lamont-Doherty Earth Observatory of Columbia University.

JELTE BOEIJENGA What is your perspective on Rebuild by Design?

KLAUS JACOB Basically it's serendipity and personal constellations and circumstances that lead to major changes. The first fact was that Sandy occurred. The second was that the U.S. Secretary of Housing and Urban Development was a New Yorker who formerly was head of the City Housing Department here. And the third serendipity was that he made a Christmas trip with his family to Berlin and stopped in the Netherlands to talk to someone, and that someone turned out to be Henk Ovink. I think it's these three circumstances—when I really think about it—that ultimately made the difference as to what happened. Because everybody in the field knew that the way the post-disaster relief and rebuilding was going on in the U.S. was faulty on so many levels that something had to change if we wanted to make a step forward into the future. So it needs circumstances and the right minds that happen to be in the right place at the right time to make a difference. And apparently Obama said yes to Henk being hired. The rest is history.

JB But that would imply that it's all pure coincidence, right? And hard to evaluate.

KJ Yes and no. It would imply that if the right people wouldn't be at the right place at the right time, it might not have happened. And it means that the right people were at the right time at the right place. And that's important. That's why elections are important, that's why the political process is important. Sure, there's a context, but it still needs these kinds of serendipities. So that's my short version of why this time things happened differently. And sure, you can say we had a different government post-Sandy compared to post-Katrina. And it happened in New York—a hub of the global information and financial network—and not in New Orleans. So people pay a little bit more attention.

> **"Smart money or political money was not going to be made available to essentially be put into a barrel without a bottom."**

But the federal government has only limited influence in the United States. It has essentially the option to put money on the table, not finance the whole thing, but enough to provide leverage, and it has the power of the pulpit. But that's pretty much it. So there are a lot of things that have to happen, also within the state and within the city, and that's the problem we still struggle with. Even if the federal government, together with generous foundations like The Rockefeller Foundation, put money on the table, that doesn't mean that the city or the state step on board with what Rebuild by Design suggested or proposed. The city has its own ideas and Rebuild by Design was an important input intellectually, for design purposes, but there are developments that are ongoing that play and interact with the modification of circumstances that Sandy brought about. They don't radically change the prior conditions, they modify them.

> **"We have a patient here, a coastal community that is not a healthy society, not a resilient, sustainable society–in the face of sustained sea level rise."**

JB So what is your evaluation of Rebuild by Design?

KJ I'm known for being critical. But not so much critical of what Rebuild by Design proposed, and of what it is still doing. I'm not against what happens right now, but if that's the only thing that happens, we're doing future generations a disservice. That's the nutshell of my criticism. We are providing a false sense of safety behind these protective measures. Practically all of them are protective rather than adaptive. As long as we stay in that mode, there comes a time when protection is insufficient. And in my mind the Netherlands haven't that figured out yet either, not for themselves, and yet protection is still sold as the solution for New Orleans. I got into big trouble after Katrina, when I wrote an editorial in the *Washington Post*, asking the tough question: "Should we rebuild New Orleans?" You should have seen the hate mail I got, it was incredible. And I understand why. That question was insensitive for the people in New Orleans that just got hit with this disaster. But I felt it was needed, particularly after I heard a speech by President Bush where he said we will rebuild New Orleans better and safer than ever before. But that was bullshit. Smart money or political money was not going to be made available to essentially be put into a barrel without a bottom. So, yes, these protective measures–including what, after Katrina, has been done in New Orleans–are important transition band-aids, but you can't heal the malaise of the body with a band-aid. And I looked at them as band-aids. They are temporarily necessary to protect the wounds and prevent further infection, but they don't heal a sick body. And unfortunately we have a patient here, a coastal community that is not a healthy society, not a resilient, sustainable society–in the face of sustained sea level rise.

JB You're an earth scientist and with that probably one of the few who look at this patient, this society, as something with a life span of hundreds of years. Is it possible for mankind to look further ahead than a lifetime?

KJ It's worth trying. And I want people to think about it. I come from a geological timescale. And I know what Mother Nature destroys in the long run. If you rely just on band-aids without having a vision of what else is needed, not to speak of how much money you need to invest in parallel into this long-term process, then I think it gets very, very serious. It becomes a moral, ethical issue of intergenerational inequity and injustice. It's not a money problem, it's not a physical problem, it becomes ultimately an ethical problem, a social problem.

> **"I come from a geological timescale. And I know what Mother Nature destroys in the long run."**

Early on, years before Sandy, we had the Dutch consulate and many of the Dutch companies with a lot of expertise, proposing barriers in New York City. And I characterized this essentially as an old technology that worked during times when there was no or very little sea level rise. Because if we have this barrier, and sea level gets up to the point where it's comparable with what we had with Sandy—let's say six, seven feet and higher, so that's by the end of the century— we ultimately still have to do everything that we would have to do without the barriers: walls around Manhattan and around the Bronx, Brooklyn, Queens and Staten Island. Because if we keep the ocean out, the Hudson and Raritan Rivers can't get out to the ocean. We flood the city from behind the barriers. We can't make '*room for the river*' here. We have The Palisades and we

have Manhattan going up there, in places more than 100 feet. We can't take the mountains away. So we would have to start pumping the rivers up into the ocean, which is ridiculous. So it became clear to me—when I was thinking it through just as a common-sense geophysicist—that in the long term, barriers are no more than a temporary solution. But it was sold by short-term thinking people as the panacea, and it is not. I haven't yet seen a true vision that looks like a viable solution when we talk about 3, 6 or ultimately 10 meters of sea level rise. So we have to look for a sustainable solution which protection is not.

The problem is, we know where the climate goes, with uncertainties of course, but we know sea level rise will go up, not down. People often ask me "Why did New York City opt for the 90 percentile of the sea level rise forecast?" As part of the NPCC, the New York City Panel on Climate Change, whose existence is now part of the city law and has an obligation to make periodic forecasts, we decided to make a probabilistic forecast, not just give a low, medium and high forecast, but a 10, 30, 75 and 90 percentile forecast. And then, of course, the designers asked, "Which one should we take?" So the recommendation was to take the 90 percentile. And people asked, of course, why take the highest level, why should we pay for all this? And I said, think of it this way: if you book a flight for tomorrow with an airline that tells you, you have only a 90 percent chance of arriving, you probably wouldn't take that flight because you don't like that there's a 10 percent chance of falling out of the sky. You have to translate probabilities into simple terms like that. It becomes a didactical and educational issue how to convey these intricacies of science and risk.

JB   And from this perspective, Rebuild by Design and the projects that come out of it run the risk of being a bandage without a vision?

KJ   We discussed those things right from the outset at the research phase of Rebuild by Design. There are ultimately five options for how to prepare for sea level rise and climate change. One is protection. The second is accommodation, let the water in. But that doesn't work under all circumstances. You can raise a house on stilts but you can't do that with city blocks. The third is strategic retreat or relocation. These are the three basic modes of adaptation. The fourth mode is to try to get insurance, which is yet another nice temporary band-aid that might work until the next disaster and the premiums will have become unaffordable by normal business principles. And then the fifth one is to do nothing. Business as usual. Just let things drift and happen.
    So amongst those five, I made it my business to focus on number three: strategic retreat and relocation. Because after all, we have the luxury of topography. We don't have topography everywhere in the United States,

but in New York City we do. And we are not using this advantage in a strategic, visionary sense. What do we do with this natural asset? We have many of these high-lying neighborhoods in Brooklyn and Queens, to some degree in Upper Manhattan, in which we have a relatively low density of population. There are two to four story houses in there, many are pretty old, sometimes dilapidated housing stock. And they're important right now, because they are the affordable housing in the city. Yet in a long-term strategic sense, these are the valuable pieces of real estate, because they're safe from sea level rise as far as the eye and the mind can see: a hundred feet and higher. So these are extraordinarily valuable assets that the city has.

"In New York City we have the luxury of topography. And we are not using this advantage in a strategic, visionary sense."

And I was one of the few who emphasized the retreat from low-lying areas early on as an important option, although I know it is politically such a hot potato that even just mentioning this is almost a crime. But with Rebuild by Design, there was intellectual openness at the beginning and I wish it had been part of the implementation phase, which it did not become. But if you're a design team and you're asked to design something, you can't say: I rezone the city as my project; that's not a project you can do. So in that sense, the process of Rebuild by Design was too constrained to really get the big picture that's needed to bring about a transformation.

JB   Constrained to rebuilding instead of revisioning?

KJ   Exactly. And that's my main criticism. Not so much of the process of Rebuild by Design, but of the larger context. We still can and should do most of the things that were proposed in Rebuild by Design. They are temporarily necessary. But it needs to be pointed out that they are transitional solutions and not necessarily sustainable solutions. And I have the luxury of being here at Columbia University, to think about those things and teach my students to think about them. So dammit, that's what I do. Sure, I'm not the mayor of New York City, I'm not the secretary of HUD. So it's easy for me here to throw out these thoughts but I feel damn serious about them. And yes, we need protection, to make that very clear. Because you can't rebuild Rome in a decade. And certainly not New York City. The problem is that we still do so many things wrong that we could avoid. We still invest in our society and our infrastructure as if we wouldn't have to look beyond short-term gains, but instead work towards longer-term sustainability. We still have major developments on the waterfront. Many are unsustainable for future raised

sea levels. Some may be tolerable, but others are sheer nonsense. And New York City is not alone, it happens everywhere in this country and probably in many places around the world. And that's where I start to raise my hand and say: shouldn't we take that into account? And of course, if you raise that hand, it's–often wrongly–interpreted as a death sentence for economic development in a given area.

"We still have major developments on the waterfront. Many are unsustainable for future raised sea levels."

JB   Does that mean that Rebuild by Design didn't bring the expected change?

KJ   Yes and no. I think Rebuild by Design introduced into the post-disaster process a long overdue transformation. And as such I think it's a big, big, big step forward. After prior disasters–if I have the principles right–it was FEMA getting the big money to pay disaster relief, providing people with food, shelter, health care. And then put money into rebuilding. But the statutes as they were on the books, practically allowed rebuilding to only what was there before. Why? Because there was the sense that people might misuse the money to improve their properties. And how do you decide if something is an improvement towards resilience instead of accommodation of personal needs? So from a bean counter point of view, it was a very simple decision: you rebuild, but not beyond. That makes it very simple to decide what is allowed and what isn't. From a bureaucratic point of view that's fabulous, from a resilience point of view it's a total disaster. And that was shaken up by Rebuild by Design. And boy, that was so long overdue. So there were some very crucial decisions being made early on after Sandy, that I think will have a long-lasting effect on how we deal with disasters, whether it's hurricanes or earthquakes or anything else.

So I believe that the very existence of Rebuild by Design is probably having a huge long-term impact on how FEMA will deal with disasters. And I would not be surprised if some of the regulations that we still have on the books right now, will change. In the New York City building code, many changes have been made since. I'm not sure I can give the credit for all of those to Rebuild by Design, but I think it was a major intellectual constellation on the sky when these changes came about. Whether each of the funded projects will see the fruits from that process, I don't know, probably not. These projects will probably still have to deal with the current realities–regulations, zoning, land use, codes and standards–because they have a certain time by which they have to be completed, by which time that other process will

probably have barely started. So Rebuild by Design brought about institutional transformation, to come back to your question with a long-winded answer, but it's a slow process. Rebuild by Design initiated transformation, but I don't think it has been able to see that transformation through to anything near where it needs to be.

▲

KLAUS JACOB–"Rebuild by Design brought about institutional transformation, but it's a slow process. Rebuild by Design initiated transformation, but I don't think it has been able to see that transformation through to anything near where it needs to be."

GEORGEEN THEODORE–"In our current system the decision-making processes will always be determined by local interests. The times we are in now mean that these local decision-making processes, these local interests, can't adapt to the larger-scale problems that we face. You can't address issues related to sea level rise if you only look at the community that is on the coast: you have to take the regional approach."

Georgeen Theodore

Principal and co-founder of Interboro

What made Rebuild by Design unique from your point of view?

GEORGEEN THEODORE

Interdisciplinary collaboration is increasingly considered crucial, we see this around the world and across many initiatives, especially in academia. But while interdisciplinary collaboration is lauded and encouraged, the processes and the organizational structures to foster that collaboration, especially in large, built projects are not yet there. So Rebuild by Design was quite unique in that it took an existing, federal program of funding projects—the United States Department of Housing and Urban Development's Community Development Block Grants—but required from the get-go that the teams were hyper-interdisciplinary, international, and multi-perspectival.

"There are frankly too few opportunities outside of academia to take that kind of approach."

The Request for Qualifications didn't say: "solve this problem." It said, "Give us your team, a mix of expertise and perspectives and present your approach." This was extremely invigorating for me as a designer. Similarly, further on in the competition, the organizers didn't ask us, for example, to figure out how to create a barrier or how to stop sea level rise. The competition said, "Identify opportunities." And even though this was difficult and complicated and aggravating for many at times, I really loved that aspect of it, because I think that's the kind of thinking that is needed today. There are frankly too few opportunities outside of academia to take that kind of approach. With Rebuild by Design, this approach was there at the outset; it was in the DNA of the project. This was critical and unique and really important. I think this was a very brilliant way to do the competition. It allowed for a temporary suspension of thinking about why you can't do things—because of the rules, or regulations, or existing practices. It allowed participants, to let loose, just for a short period of time, and do something that would be unthinkable under the normal circumstances.

So our team reveled in it. We had really taken the RFQ to heart and ended up with a team that combined the best of Dutch landscape design and water engineering with American participatory design approaches. And added to this political scientists, educational experts, experts in financial and economic analysis, et cetera. So our team from the get-go was really trying to leverage this transdisciplinary approach. We brought together different experts, who were looking at large-scale, top-down planning, but who were also looking at local dynamics and conditions and trying to bring that together. Our project really came out of the potentials but also the productive frictions that emerge when you have people with these different perspectives.

JB   What stands out in the process of the competition?

GT   You really have to look at the process as a double-edged sword. Because everything that is a strength in the process is also a challenge. The competition was a call to address regional resiliency, and that's good, but it also asked to actually propose design interventions that were implementable, to get something done within the short term. If we go back to the process—in stage 2 you had to identify the opportunities, and in stage 3 you had the assignment of one opportunity to develop. At the end of stage 3 you had to have a client or a partner to support the project. So in the end, the projects that we advocated were projects that we had the support for on the part of the local governments or local leadership. But that doesn't mean that that's going to be the most impactful project. So this is the double-edged sword: that which is the most implementable, given the local, political dynamics, is not necessarily going to be the most impactful. The projects that we pushed for reflect this balancing. You could say that this process was visionary, it was innovative, groundbreaking, but at the same time it was really like real life, because it was full of all the kinds of compromises that any kind of design project has. That's a funny element of the process.

JB   Can we see this dilemma in your project as well?

GT   I would say that our project and the design opportunities that our team identified always reflected this dilemma. We as a team were always seeking for a long-term regional strategy, and at the same time looking to identify locally rooted, catalytic and implementable projects. Both of these perspectives are necessary, and working with both of them simultaneously caused a lot of healthy friction. Should we have exclusively pursued the large-scale strategy, we would not have won any funding because it wouldn't have been implementable given our political context. And at the same time, if we would have just done smaller projects that were locally rooted, that could be realized in the short term, but maybe weren't framed by a larger regional perspective, it would not have been as successful either. So we made a comprehensive regional plan, five different strategies and for each of these strategies we identified implementable projects that could jumpstart the larger strategy. And those are the ones where we really were in a race to find people to help support it. But these projects were all different. Some of them would be very impactful, but very expensive and hard to do in the regulatory context. Other ones are easier to do, maybe less expensive, but they have less impact.

I'm sure people will say that a big failure of Rebuild by Design was that the grantees or the stakeholders came in way too late in the process. What happened, was that the projects for funding were selected, but the people who said that they supported it weren't necessarily the grantees, the cities and states awarded the CDBG-DR money. So the governor's office had to take this project on, but they didn't initially identify it. That again is this double-edged sword dynamic I mentioned before. Had the grantee been responsible for identifying and initially developing the project, the grantee would never have come up with the strategy we developed. Our interdisciplinary and collaborative project would have never come out of the traditional method. But at the same time, because we had that critical distance from the decision-making processes that usually produces a certain type of project, we were able to develop something that was different and hopefully more impactful and innovative, more replicable and more valuable. But that distance with the grantee also meant that the grantee didn't have meaningful participation in the definition of the project, but was nonetheless responsible for implementing it. It's possible that a grantee could not be invested or even interested in innovative, interdisciplinary collaboration. That's a foundational problem.

"That which is the most implementable, given the local, political dynamics, is not necessarily going to be the most impactful."

JB That makes the process extremely vulnerable, so it seems.

GT Yes, one risk is that the grantee might decide to drop the project or let it die a slow death because they were not invested in the ideas of the project in the first. Or the grantee wants to continue "business as usual," and has no interest in innovation and/or interdisciplinary collaboration. Another risk here is that the grantees will get their allocation and do the project and that will be it, without realizing the potential for replication. So for example, in our Living with the Bay project, we identified the Mill River as an area to focus on, because it was replicable, because there are so many other similar rivers emptying into a bay. And these rivers are tied into the system of storm water management, tied into the sewage system, they're tied into the ecology of the region, fish and plant life that are associated with it, and it's also a recreational resource. So it's something that if you can do it here, you could then replicate it elsewhere. And we're learning and we have learned so much about how to make this better. Will we have a chance to repeat it somewhere else? This is a question. Will there be other programs to fund other similar projects in the future? Right now there's nothing, so that's a challenge.

JB   What do you think will be the lasting change of Rebuild by Design?

JB   And Rebuild by Design changed this?

GT   One of the biggest drivers in this process was the money. And it was absolutely essential that there was this money allocated by the federal government to move through this process. The traditional process of funding and implementation through community development block grants in the U.S. really reflects on our federal system, in that the federal government doesn't want to tell localities what to do. The localities, that is the grantees, get their funding, and then they can do what they want to do with it. On the one hand, you can understand why those principles exist, because people who live in a place know many of their issues and challenges better than somebody from the outside. But you can also see that there are some things, like when we think about climate change or access to education, in which our system of local governance fails. When a local municipality elects its own local official, that local official has to respond to her electorate. If she thinks beyond her electorate, then she's going to lose her position. In our current system, leadership, and the decision-making processes of local leaders, will always be determined by local interests. The times we are in now mean that these local decision-making processes, these local interests, can't adapt to the larger-scale problems that we face. Which are not only about climate change. You can't address issues related to sea level rise if you only look at the community that is on the coast: you have to take the regional approach.

GT   Yes. This project was really trying to break new ground in the way that our government works. In terms of rebuilding after disasters, but also really in terms of these relationships between regional and local. The way the money has always gone through the community development block grant process, is that ultimately the localities decide how to spend it. And somehow Rebuild by Design figured out how to do that in a different way. There were some strings attached to this cycle of grants. So this chunk of money is going to be working its way through the system for a couple of years. And although this is very, very challenging, when I think about it optimistically, I would say that that is the great success of Rebuild by Design. Even though it was a one-time competition, that money is there and the projects are there. So people have to figure out what to do with it. The projects have to be pushed through the different systems of contracting and implementing; the localities now have to check back in with HUD. It doesn't mean that it's always going to be perfect, there will be a lot of failures along the way, but at the same time they simply cannot do it the way that they did it before. So they have to adjust and they have to adapt. That's a learning process and a process of innovation, because new things have to happen.

▲

GEORGEEN THEODORE—"Even though it was a one-time competition, that money is there and the projects are there. So people have to figure out what to do with it. It doesn't mean that it's always going to be perfect, there will be a lot of failures along the way, but at the same time they simply cannot do it the way that they did it before. That's a learning process and a process of innovation, because new things have to happen."

PART III
Researching the Region July—November 2013

When I wake up on the morning of Friday, July 19, I check my email immediately. Today is the deadline for submissions to our Request for Qualifications. For the past month, we have been broadcasting news about Rebuild by Design, inviting teams of designers to tell us why they are qualified to participate in our competition. Today, we will find out if what we are doing appeals to them.

There are two entries.

I had promised Shaun fifty entries, hoping we'd get seventy-five. Now we have raised $4.45 million dollars, we have the President of the United States counting on us—and we have two teams interested. That's the same number we had last night, before I went to bed.

I get up and bike to work. It's early, I tell myself, but I am nervous. Shaun calls me later in the morning. We'll get more, I promise, but I don't really believe it when I say it. Slowly, the tally climbs. By lunchtime, we have some thirty submissions. Better, but not great. Then, in the afternoon, the pace picks up. Entries begin to pour in. By the close of business, we have

148 teams who want to participate. This is more than a relief, it's a reason for a party! This level of interest is unprecedented.

My team will work through the weekend, and I'm thrilled to have so many options to choose from and can't wait to read every one of the proposals. I have prepared carefully for this moment. Friday evening and Saturday, my team technically evaluates and categorizes all the entries, dividing them among twenty-eight reviewers drawn from the task force agencies. Each submission will be evaluated by a mix of specialists: policy experts, designers, scientists and engineers, representatives of different agencies in the task force. Every reviewer receives a subset of entries plus assessment forms with the criteria from the design brief, and has until Tuesday evening to submit their reviews. My D.C. team will sort everything on Tuesday. On Wednesday, we will gather with the entire review commit-

tee, chaired by the National Endowment for the Arts (NEA), to select about twenty teams to discuss with Shaun.

I deliberately made the first stage of the competition a Request for Qualifications rather than a Request for Proposals. We need talent before solutions, and I am seeking a wide

"The reason we formed a team with OLIN was because their project was completely, totally aligned with the mission of the 21st century university: taking what we learn, integrating it, making it actionable, to achieve positive social impact. Our university is willing to step up and say that. Penn is inclusive. We integrate knowledge and innovate around the research that we undertake to achieve social good. That's what our mission statement says. In terms of the world of design, that means you have to work hard on your research, you have to develop your clients' capacity and you have to be proactive about assembling the arguments and the resources to get the project done. There were how many times at Skidmore, Owings & Merill, that I put a beautiful drawing on the wall and somebody said, 'Let's build it'? Zero. You always have to have the narrative. You have to find the champion. And that does not always fall to the designer; sometimes it falls to the mayor, sometimes it falls to a foundation or philanthropy. But I do think that part of the designers' job is to catalyze it where it doesn't exist. And to do that,

Marilyn
Jordan Taylor

Professor of Architecture
and Urban Design and
Dean of the University
of Pennsylvania School
of Design (PennDesign)
from 2008 to 2016

117

you can't just say, 'Well, it's a really good idea, and these are going to be all of its benefits,' you have to say, 'Oh, but we do not have an agency that is going to do that, so we need a special purpose authority. What kind? How does it raise money?' There are a whole set of things which are not what you learn in architecture and not what you learn in landscape, but when you spend enough of your life working on projects, you just inherently say, 'It has got to be part of my assignment since there's nobody else there doing it.' That's why I think design fits this larger university mission."

range of expertise. We asked teams to pick a focus area: coastal communities, high-density urban environments, ecological and waterbody networks or a catch-all category. They had to describe their approach to Rebuild by Design, explaining how they would tackle the region's complexity and deal with the diversity of stakeholders, the scale and the need for innovation. We were seeking distinctive approaches to resilience that addressed the process; interdisciplinary research; the spatial impact of ecological, societal and economic development; workable, location-specific design solutions; and building local and regional coalitions.

On June 24, our twenty-eight reviewers, representing twenty-three agencies, convene from around the country at our task force office, where Jason Schupbach of the National Endowment for the Arts in Washington D.C. chairs the day's

Talent ⟶	Research ⟶	Design ⟶	Implementation
Gather the talent of the world to work with the talent of the Sandy-affected region. Design teams are selected comprising a diverse set of complementary skills and approaches.	Establish the broadest possible understanding of the region's vulnerabilities to future risks and interdependencies, to enhance resilience. Research is collaborative across teams and focuses on typologies as well as locations. Each team presents three to five "design opportunities".	Teams gather diverse local stakeholders into community coalitions, with whom they co-design implementable solutions that have support from the communities and local governments.	HUD allocates disaster recovery funds to city and state governments for the implementation of the projects' first stages. Governments and community stakeholders work together to build the projects.

proceedings. Jason has a lot of experience with this sort of thing, but he tells me he has never seen such overwhelmingly high quality in the entries. Among the firms and practices that have made submissions, nearly thirty countries are represented. Many include Dutch team members, which does not surprise me but is gratifying all the same. Most entries come from the U.S., with more than half the states represented. Ambition is written all over the submissions. It's clear that the contenders grasp the complexity and the possibilities inherent in Rebuild by Design. They present sharp and straightforward analyses, full of insight about how to influence the system. No one presents solutions—that's premature. What I asked for—and apparently got—in these submissions is design thinking in action: bringing everything together in the context of politics, place, economy and ecology, unraveling complexity to reveal innovative solutions. I am deeply heartened. The quality of the work represented in these 148 entries, evident so early in our process, tells me that Rebuild by Design is on track to become something truly special.

The atmosphere in the room is electric. Every proposal has been reviewed by four individuals, and as we consider each, they weigh in. They are young and old, from different agencies and different disciplines, with different backgrounds. The result is a rich, informed deliberation as we cut the submissions in half on the first round. On subsequent rounds, we cut again, and again. I hate to see some teams go, just as I know others do, but this is a juried process. Our goal is to get to twenty teams I can present to Shaun Donovan. He will select the ten we invite to work with us in the actual design competition. By the end of the day, we are down to twenty-one teams. That will do. All of us know that any of these contenders will be a good choice.

Four days later, a Sunday, I sit with Shaun on the porch of his home. We go through each entry carefully. I know Shaun doesn't want to be rushed. Why this one? Why not? We work our way through each offering, and then I leave the proposals with him. In the coming days we discuss them over again and in the end, alone, he will make his list of ten.

Can We Work Together?

At the beginning of the second week of August, I telephone the winners. A week later, they are in Washington D.C., gathered at a celebratory dinner. Their teams comprise many members, but we will come to shorthand them as:

BIG TEAM

HR&A ADVISORS, INC., WITH COOPER, ROBERTSON & PARTNERS

INTERBORO TEAM

MIT CAU + ZUS + URBANISTEN

OMA TEAM

PENNDESIGN / OLIN

SASAKI / RUTGERS / ARUP

SCAPE / LANDSCAPE ARCHITECTURE

WB UNABRIDGED WITH YALE ARCADIS

WXY / WEST 8

The news is still fresh for these people who have flown to New York from all over the world, and their excitement is palpable. Shaun is present, and we have a great casual party—a prelude to the unknown. Tomorrow we begin work, and nobody here tonight understands what that means.

The next morning, Friday, I set the stage for them this way: "Congratulations! The competition is over." And I mean it. The representatives of the task force agencies, and ultimately Shaun in his capacity as chair of the Sandy Task Force, selected these ten teams from 148 contenders. They are here to work not only with us, but with each other. "From now on, all of you, all ten teams, are the winners. You'll be competing not against each other but against the highest standard. The better the result, the greater the chance that your project will be implemented, and that goes for everyone."

That same day, we begin our first two days of on-the-ground research at the Lower East Side, in Hoboken and Jersey City. Almost every week for the next two months, we take extended, organized field trips to affected communities in such places as Asbury Park, Bridgeport and Red Hook. We meet with mayors, city agencies and community groups. The next Friday we regroup, and as the debriefing progresses, I can see that everyone has a much better understanding of what Rebuild by Design is about. I sense a dawning realization of what we are to accomplish together—not only of what we expect of the teams, but what we offer them: a facilitated process, two months of joint site visits, discussions, and rich access to knowledge, organizations, people and peers, full of opportunities to learn and connect.

Three hands go up with the same question: "Can we work together? Do the competition criteria allow this?" I am so gratified by this query. "Yes, you can! In fact, that is the whole point—you have to! This is precisely what I meant when I said, 'the competition is over.'" If we really are going to unravel the complexity of the region, we must collaborate, and not as members of separate teams but as one coalition of experts. Each team is made up of professionals with complementary expertise and competencies: ecology, infrastructure, housing, water, you name it. To facilitate cooperation, the Rebuild by Design staff groups the specialists from different teams together. As the research proceeds, these groups will work together in their

"Perhaps the oddest thing about the Rebuild By Design competition was that it never really felt like a competition. The process we collectively developed was set up to foster collaboration all around. For instance, in the research phase, members of all ten teams (and staff from the four partnered not-for-profit organizations) spent several months visiting more than thirty different communities around the Northeast to speak with people about their experiences in the storm and its aftermath. By having all the design teams mixed on the busses, it quickly became a collegial atmosphere instead of an actively competitive one. I have not seen that happen before in a competition. Some of the design teams may have had pretty clear ideas of what they wanted their final projects to be even before getting on the bus, other teams perhaps less so. However, in each case their projects were shaped (further) by the conversations with the communities. The question to all involved was always: 'Can we actually make a project together?' As, in the end, every successful project requires chemistry."

David
van der Leer

Executive Director of
Van Alen Institute

Teams on the ground on the Lower East Side, Manhattan

area of expertise so that the learning is truly collective. With Eric Klinenberg and Sam Carter from the Institute for Public Knowledge, we agree to compile all the research results into a single analysis, made by all and available to all. Everyone will know what everyone has learned.

The Risk of Two Governments

Back in the early spring (it seems so long ago!), the first draft of Hurricane Sandy Task Force Report had been issued with Rebuild by Design buried in an appendix. Those were uncertain days for this project; we have come a long way since then. By August, our competition is funded and we are deep into the research phase. We have been working on a parallel track to complete the final draft of the task force report, called the Hurricane Sandy Rebuilding Strategy, which has gone through many iterations. As senior advisor to Shaun, I am deeply involved with the writing team. As before, the negotiations around which recommendations will be included, and under what terms, are deeply political and go down to the wire. In the end, the report, released by the White House on August 9, includes sixty-nine recommendations. Much of what we propose is already underway. Only a few of these recommendations are of high priority for the task force, requiring political management and protection and continuing federal involvement for the next eighteen months. This time, instead of being in the appendix, Rebuild by Design is right up there in the top five recommendations.

We have transformed Rebuild by Design from being almost forgotten to being the focus of intense attention and status. That attention brings pressure, and I welcome it, for we need politics at the core of Rebuild by Design. Political pressure often increases the fear of making mistakes and pushes policy makers to hunker down, yet fear cannot drive us. As design thinkers, we embrace the idea of making mistakes and learning from them. Risk and reward are closely connected in Rebuild by Design.

Of course, not everything I wanted ended up in the final task force report. A proposal to assess the task force's process and share lessons learned throughout the federal government fell by the wayside. Nevertheless, we did get a small anchor for change into the report: "HUD will, in collaboration with

---

AUG 19, 2013.   THE BROOKINGS INSTITUTION,
WASHINGTON D.C.

A Statement on the Hurricane Sandy Rebuilding Task Force Report

"Today the Obama administration's Hurricane Sandy Rebuilding Task Force issued important guidelines for the expenditure of federal funds in the service of local recovery visions and priorities. In the wake of recent high-profile natural disasters, cities, metropolitan areas and regions across the country are beginning to embrace resilience as the new planning norm. Resilience strategies represent a new approach to how cities plan, design, build and manage their communities (and particularly essential infrastructure services) in the face of a complex, uncertain and ever-changing future.

The Hurricane Sandy Rebuilding Strategy reinforces this bottom-up approach and shows how the federal government can be a reliable, supportive partner. The strategy shows an unprecedented commitment to coordination across federal agencies and collaboration between the federal, state and local governments and key local constituencies. Instead of establishing new programs with restrictive statutory provisions, the task force recommends (and has already begun to implement) new locally-driven solutions through innovative design competitions and added flexibility for communities to decide how funds can be spent within and across jurisdictions.

As Shaun Donovan, the secretary of the U.S. Department of Housing and Urban Development and chair of the Task Force, wrote in the transmittal of the report: "Local governments and community leaders are the front lines of disaster recovery, and it is the job of the Federal Government to have their back by supporting their efforts, providing guidance when necessary and delivering resources to help them fulfill their needs." The Rebuilding Strategy represents a critical step forward in how the federal government helps states, regions and localities recover in the aftermath of natural disasters. It also, more broadly, shows a federal commitment to localism and regionalism that has implications for a wide range of domestic policies."

Metropolitan Policy Program director Bruce Katz and senior fellow Robert Puentes

philanthropic organizations, evaluate the Rebuild by Design competition process using the process of this competition as an inspiration, and research the possibilities of applying 'regional resilience by design' in other regions across the nation." In short, the promise to scale up and replicate across the United States is there. We only need to make it happen.

The Infrastructure Resiliency Guidelines we proposed in the spring also made the final cut. This is significant, as they must be applied to all federal investments in the Sandy recovery. They will affect, for the better, the way existing federal infrastructure funding processes are executed. A few weeks earlier, President Obama's counselor, John Podesta, had joined us at a task force meeting, where he warned us of the dangers of creating two parallel governments: one that is very good at disaster response, efficient and effective, and a second, established government that keeps making the same mistakes and keeps failing. I think about this often, for this repeated failure afflicts governments worldwide. Time and again, policy makers and bureaucrats rise to the occasion and develop innovative processes, only to fall back into old patterns after a crisis passes. How do we change culture so that those innovations are embraced and baked into the existing ways of doing things? I see this problem in my own work: of all the people who witnessed the task force at work, only a few embraced its approach and its work ethic. Most tolerated it as an exception, a temporary threat to power and turf that would pass by.

Does Rebuild by Design face the same risk? That is, will we innovate, developing an effective approach to complexity and risk—and then revert to the way things were before? If we fail to use experiments like Rebuild by Design as opportunities to change how we deal with challenges, we will not only fall back again next time, but we will fall harder, with more devastating consequences.

Yet I do see small signs of lasting impact. People sense the opportunity to do things differently, to incrementally change standard operating procedures and slowly, step by step, make change from within. This is potentially transformative, for when people change, culture changes. Every step we take is new, and that in itself is a big win.

TOO BIG
for Our
Systems

Create a Free Place

Create a Free Place

We need a different culture of working, together.
Real change comes from outside. The enormous
complexity calls for room to experiment, reflect
and innovate. Time and space where we can
step outside existing interests and frameworks,
legitimized by the huge challenges ahead.
Challenges which can never be met by our current
approach and conditions, our agreed-upon
procedures and institutions, rooted as these are
in the past. We need room to experiment, in which
we tie government responsibilities to the strength
of initiatives in our communities, in academia,
by activist groups and by our businesses and
investors. Room to take risks, make mistakes and
learn, to set change in motion.

Create a Free Place

This experiment requires a safe place that frees us from the "not allowed" and "won't work" attitudes, based on yesterday's experiences. A place where we can collaborate, where it's all about people, not positions, on a level playing field, space where we can get away from solidified relations and accepted roles. A place where everyone can be vulnerable, where government and communities or citizens and corporations are not on opposite sides, where everyone can change roles and positions. A place where disagreement and even conflict can grow into understanding and better solutions. Here we can organize a truly inclusive and transparent process, rooted in trust and collaboration, a process where individual vulnerability is respected and can grow into a collective force for change.

Create a Free Place

Such an experiment is temporary and probably dedicated to a single challenge or event, specifically managed and with a distinctive position. An exception to the rule. President Obama's Hurricane Sandy Rebuilding Task Force was one such exception. But what's next? Do we quickly return to our initial positions or do we exploit the exception to learn and sustainably change the system? Do we continue with two systems—the innovative and effective exception in response to our crises alongside the existing system which fails with every unconventional circumstance— or do we use the power of the experiment for an incremental process of development and improvement? We must experiment, practice and test, but also evaluate. We must learn and incorporate those lessons into our day-to-day work. We must not only respond to unique events but also invest in the future to bring lasting change. Change that is both institutional and cultural. Change that is engraved in our hearts and minds and entrenched in our processes, organizations and agreements. Only then can we work towards a resilient society. A society not only capable of responding to disruption and disasters but a society that is prepared, ready for the future together.

We go through several personnel shifts. Laurel Blatchford steps down and Marion McFadden becomes the task force CEO. Kevin Bush takes another job and Scott Davis, an experienced post-disaster policy advisor, becomes HUD's first point of contact. Amy Chester joins the team as Rebuild by Design's project manager and, with Sam Carter, makes a flying start on the research stage.

Every other week, we travel with the design teams—in New York City, in New Jersey, on Long Island, Staten Island, in Connecticut—and we meet everyone there is to meet. Now Rebuild by Design is all about asking questions, questions and more questions. Can the teams have full insights in all the data, have access to everything and ask anything? The grantees have questions, too: What are the teams up to, what do they want, why do they want to speak with the governor? Those of us on the task force are working with Shaun Donovan on the idea of a national competition and thinking about the future. What happens after our competition is over?

"Hurricane Sandy created a space to think big. There was a willingness to test new things. It's not always that case with government, so you need to know when to recognize those moments, and be prepared. Like in a political campaign, you don't know when the moment is going to happen, but then the opponent screws up by eating pizza with a fork, and then the opposition will act quickly to take advantage of it by saying, 'Oh my goodness, he's not a real New Yorker!' You always have to be ready, knowing how you will take advantage when you see an opening. Generally, government shoos away from big ideas because they're too big, too complicated or they cannot be accomplished before the next election. But they're not too big. A big idea is actually just a bunch of little components put together. These big ideas don't have to be scary, they don't have to be 'too big.' You need to figure out what are the many hundreds of little steps, or even just the first few that you have to do to make it happen. However, you can't start something like Rebuild by Design by mapping everything out for the next eight

Amy Chester

Project Manager and later Managing Director of Rebuild by Design months and say, 'This is the plan'—it would never work. We had a general idea, but we were really building it as it went along. And as any big effort, it took on the personalities of the people who worked on it every single day, according to our individual understandings, personal experiences and what we thought would make a great process. And if you just do the work, you're learning from what you're doing, you're adapting and next time you do it differently. During the competition, the design teams pushed for certain things, and we adapted. And then we pushed for certain things, and they adapted. It was a big adaptation process for everyone over these eight or nine months: us, the design teams, federal government, cities and states. And as a result, everyone has changed. There's no doubt that every single person in this process changed and was impacted by this process. You have to be agile and responsive and you have to not lower your aspirations because someone else's are lower. It's about thinking big and not letting the regular system's inertia stop you."

Collectively, we create a beehive, an ants' nest of activity, chaos with just enough organization to make it work. Our networks and our influence are growing. We are on the radar of a growing number of people. Everything is political. Do we truly mean to collaborate, people wonder, or will there be negotiations first? Trust is building, but it is still not deep or robust. Will the design competition produce the best result for one, or the most success for all?

Henk Ovink with the design teams to tour the Bay Park Sewage Treatment Plant on Long Island

We go to Asbury Park—the fabled Jersey Shore town where Bruce Springsteen, Jon Bon Jovi and other New Jersey musicians launched their careers at The Stone Pony—and meet across the street from the music venue to listen to the stories of community members, activists, business owners and government officials. This is a sweet little town, divided by a railway line that separates the wealthy from the vulnerable. Its famous boardwalk has been devastated by Sandy. There are not very many cars in the parking lots. Months after Sandy, this place is hurting.

We listen carefully to the stories, very carefully, and really take it in. We don't have much to offer yet in terms of answers, solutions or promises, and that can make these meetings hard. For now we are here to learn: What happened? What went wrong? What went right? Here's what we read in the reports—but what was your experience? What, exactly, is the problem as you see it? This is legitimate fact-finding, and the knowledge we collect forms crucial building blocks. But some

"The early research phase of Rebuild by Design encouraged us to look at all the impacts of climate change on urban areas, taking the time to diagnose the actual problems and thoroughly understand the risks at hand–and this process was transformative. Design competitions usually provide a defined program or problem statement, such as a vacant site positioned for new development or an infrastructure investment. In the case of Rebuild by Design, neither the program nor the specific problem were defined, leaving teams the latitude to identify problems and come up with creative solutions. That said, we knew the general outline of the problem from the outset, broadly speaking: for many cities and populations across the country and around the world, there is vast and increasing risk related to climate change, and solutions that rely wholly on government funding will not be financially sustainable over time. So, our team worked to uncover new solutions that could utilize non-traditional funding streams, supported by either private investment or innovative public financing

Jamie Springer

Partner at HR&A
Advisors

structures, to incrementally transform the long-term resilience of people, places and communities. Our big question was: what are relatively low-cost but high-impact things a city can do to protect at-risk property and populations without or in advance of major capital investments? Rebuild by Design allowed our team to tackle this question, innovating our thinking and design processes and building consensus along the way."

attendees view those of us representing the federal government as part of the problem. We have to be accountable—if not for what happened, then at least for getting something done, now. If we can't do it, they feel, we should send them the money "and we'll do the rest."

At our next stop, in Keansburg, New Jersey, this tension is drawn in even sharper relief. We go to a soup kitchen to volunteer and to listen to the stories of people who lost their homes and still have no place to go. While our presence is encouraging to some of these people, many are despairing, tearful and at wit's end. They don't really trust us to help, and they also believe the feds are not helping enough. After all, half of the homes destroyed in Keansburg and elsewhere in the region were not even inside flood zones, according to federal flood maps. If the government couldn't even get that right, how will it get anything else right? From the perspective of Keansburg, Washington D.C. is a dysfunctional squabble between Republicans and Democrats, between the federal government and the states. It doesn't seem like anyone can be trusted. If someone lost a house, they want it back. If they lost a business, they want it back. Never mind if they lost a husband, a daughter or a friend. The people in this soup kitchen couldn't care less about a blue-eyed bald guy from the Netherlands talking about working together, about building back innovatively, about climate change and the future.

With all the misery that is here, hardly anybody is interested in innovating. Just give me back what I had, they say. Just that. Don't invent the future; restore the past.

This may be the most important, biggest challenge Rebuild by Design faces. In the moment of a crisis, resistance

to change is high—but so is the opportunity to do things better. Our task is to bridge the gap between the resistance we feel everywhere and the possibilities we know are inherent in this crisis. We feel it here in Keansburg, and in Asbury Park, and in other wounded communities we visit. We see it in the way Congress agreed on a recovery bill without adequately considering the future, and in FEMA's funding approach to rebuilding what was lost without taking into account the future challenges climate change will bring. Resistance is endemic, baked into a collective attachment to the way things have always been done. How do we move beyond the longing for the past and memory of what was toward what could be?

This is not some abstract exercise. This is not an ordinary design competition to develop flood protection infrastructure. This is about real people and real despair. Everyone involved in Rebuild by Design understands this reality now, if they did not before we visited Keansburg. We can create a huge win with this project—or fail the people in this room. What we are trying to do will not work without their understanding of what we are trying to accomplish. Many of them are in denial—either because of conservatism or fear or both—about climate change and rising seas and what the future will bring. We must bridge the gap from where they are to where we are. How will we bring them along? How can we confront what

Carrie Grassi
Interview p.226

"Rebuild by Design wasn't just a design competition, it was a mutual process of education that both the designers and the communities embarked on together."

they see as government underperformance, if not outright failure, in a way that addresses their despair and opens their eyes to the need to step into the future?

The HR&A team develops a first-pass analysis, revealing that small businesses here have no access to aid money that is theirs but isn't reaching them. Most of them rent their spaces, so they can't receive Build It Back funding. They don't have their own resources to invest, and their regular sources of income—tourists—have largely vanished in the wake of the storm and its devastation. So how do we help them not only recover but also be prepared for the next disaster? This is the sort of wicked problem that demands all the stakeholders be in the room to develop a solution, from landlords to government experts. Confronted by the real problems real people are experiencing, we can see how essential inclusiveness is to finding solutions.

We continue our weekly rhythm of two- and three-day journeys to different areas affected by Sandy, such as this one to the Jersey Shore, always asking questions. The meetings are

Teams on the ground in Bridgeport, Connecticut

a public show of who is involved, from the governor's office down to local officials, and this is important because eventually these people will be responsible for implementing whatever Rebuild by Design develops.

Each trip reveals new learnings and new insights. On Manhattan's Lower East Side, we hear stories of elderly and vulnerable apartment dwellers who were stranded when flood-waters cut off power to their elevators. We sit with activists, building administrators, in Red Hook the IKEA representatives who are providing temporary accommodations for the displaced, and ask the same questions. What happened? Why do you think it did? What is the situation? How can we understand the social and physical dynamics of this place? We think about strategies for changing not only the infrastructure but the culture and politics that create and sustain it. We look for connections with other places we have visited. What is similar? What is personal and uniquely local?

The Richness of Complexity

The Regional Plan Association, the Municipal Art Society and the Van Alen Institute, who are collectively preparing the design stage, want to take part in the research stage that Institute for Public Knowledge is leading. I feel this makes sense, because they know the region in different ways than IPK, and also because if they understand what is happening in the research stage they will do a better job of preparing and running the design stage. So they join in this multifaceted, cross-disciplinary involvement that drives our beehive, our ants' nest. We have ten teams at work, each consisting of at least four or five organizations, supported by a core team led by Amy Chester; a whole network of researchers that IPK has assembled; six foundations who are naturally curious about our progress; our four partners; the federal government (with HUD at the forefront plus a dozen other agencies directly connected, including the White House); and the grantees, mayors, communities and more.

Nobody said collaboration is easy, and right now it certainly is not. Who is in charge? Who isn't but should be? When, where and how to connect? Who is missing? Why? This structured chaos is critical to success. In the safety of their organizations, people tend to work in silos. We are here to break silos apart. We need synergy so all things really can come together. In-depth understanding comes from specializing, but impact comes from making connections. The answer is not binary, it is everything at once: deep dives plus making connections; community work plus laboratory research; political debates plus visionary narratives.

I know that Rebuild by Design is not a blueprint. Everything is different everywhere in the world. But I also know this open, inclusive and comprehensive perspective that embraces physical, social and governance complexity is critical for whatever we do and wherever we are if we are to tackle our future's most challenging crises with relevant results. That is how we will produce impactful projects that inspire, that we can evaluate, replicate and scale up. Resilience and integration only have value if you really open up the process for integrating all relationships, in particular with stakeholders who are less outspoken, visible or active. We have to immerse ourselves fully in complexity, and of course this creates the kind of chaos we are experiencing now in Rebuild by Design. Too much chaos leads to failure. Running the beehive demands a different type of management and different organizational skills. We are learning them as we let complexity lead us forward.

A Safe Place

Collaboration between the teams grows. At each site visit, they present interim research results so they can learn and reflect. But how much sharing is too much? During our visit to Asbury Park, the MIT team unveils stunningly beautiful maps they have developed. In only a few weeks, they have charted the entire region and its vulnerabilities across most of the challenges we've identified: physical, social, network and so on. Immediately, the other teams ask if they can have access to the maps.

Georgeen Theodore
Interview p.110

"Rebuild by Design allowed for a temporary suspension of thinking about why you can't do things–because of the rules, or regulations, or existing practices. It allowed participants to let loose, just for a short period of time, and do something that would be unthinkable under the normal circumstances"

This is the first real test of our collaboration. Are we really working together? Will the teams truly benefit from each other's efforts? We agreed at the start that the research stage was a collective effort, but now the tension underlying that is out in the open. Does this agreement imply everyone shares everything? Do the teams only share the data, background and findings they gather, or do they also share the work they create from that data? The first certainly makes sense—otherwise what's the point of collaborating? But we also agree that a team's conclusion, anything that clearly has their fingerprints on it, is personal to the team. In light of that, we agree that the MIT maps are outside the sharing pool yet the data behind these is open to all. We are feeling our way toward the limits of collaboration inside a competition.

The collective learning is an iterative process, a relentless series of meetings and site visits that increases engagement with federal officials, local bureaucrats, residents and activists. Insights lead to new sets of questions, new needs and return visits. Sometimes we gather at our headquarters and IPK, but mostly we gather on the ground: in Hoboken, Staten Island, the Jersey Shore, Long Island, Red Hook, Hunts Point, Bridgeport. Each trip draws together a different constellation of individuals who ask questions, learn, explore and exploit their professional creativity in ways they normally cannot.

TOO BIG
to Go Alone

Be Radically Inclusive

Be Radically Inclusive

To tackle today's challenges, we need everyone:
governments, businesses, scientists, NGOs,
community leaders and activists. This is
not because good plans otherwise fail in
implementation, although they do. Rather, without
this coalition, we won't get to the real problems in
the first place. The perspective of the man who
has lost his daughter is just as relevant as that of
the scientist who knows what caused the disaster,
the designer who knows what the solution looks
like, the official who creates the policy and the
politician who makes the decisions. This calls
for radical inclusiveness. The community has
different needs than the government or the
investor; science conducts a different analysis
than policy makers do; federal politics differ from
local dynamics. If we ignore these differences, we
fail to get to the heart of the challenges. It is only
with everyone involved—all part of the problem as
much as of the solution—that the comprehensive
approach is not an academic exercise but is
rooted in society's needs and helps us arrive at
transformative solutions.

Be Radically Inclusive

These coalitions are all about people, not positions. The task is not to create alliances of like-minded people but partnerships that bring maximum diversity, with room for different perspectives and interests. Such collaboration requires an open and inviting process, driven not by control but by trust and transparency. This can be chaotic, but these partnerships are not aimed at making the process simpler. They are designed to enrich it. Real collaboration doesn't require control but makes room to invest in one another. It incorporates freedom and allows for maximum interaction. So the door is always open; no one is ever too late to join. That was Rebuild by Design's motto, its culture, right from the beginning. Real change only happens if we start together, proceeding from what we don't know, from our questions and desires, not our preconceived answers and demands. Then we can create together, learn together, evaluate together, improve and perform better the next time.

Be Radically Inclusive

Within these coalitions, negotiation makes way
for collaboration. Whereas negotiation always
leads to an average—with everyone giving in a bit
until a middle ground is reached—collaboration is
aimed not at the average but at maximum value.
Negotiation is rooted in the idea of winners and
losers; collaboration is driven by a determination
to add value to all. Collaboration embraces
difference and surprise, allows us to invest in
each other and generate impact through synergy.
It takes everyone to change everything.

The importance of the task force for Rebuild by Design becomes apparent. Not only can the competition grow beneath the wings of the task force, but the task force itself can insure collaboration between departments and agencies. We need that collaboration, we need that knowledge of what can or cannot be done, what the policy is, what the law says, what needs to change. Rebuild by Design is a skunk works inside the political–institutional reality of the task force, and this is perfect. If we were operating on our own, we would lose touch with the institutions of government, and that would represent a failure. The task force legitimizes Rebuild by Design and keeps us connected to the people whom we must call upon for help. We may be an odd duck, but we are at least familiar to them now. They are not surprised when we call them for a workshop or a meeting. They show up, prepared and ready to engage, to share their knowledge, expertise and ideas, to reflect on the teams' work and the process of moving forward. They keep our experiment connected to the real world.

Rebuild by Design is growing into a safe place for all involved. We have agreed on the acceptable level of chaos that

"In the U.S., government does not have a good mechanism to work with communities. In New York City, it just doesn't work. We have an Environmental Impact Statement process, for which you have to have a public hearing, and government has to state at the end of the document how they responded to comments and not actually change anything; it doesn't work. We have hearings on the Metropolitan Transportation Authority capital plan where each person gets three minutes to talk into a microphone at a dais of the Board of Directors, who are not paying attention–they are reading papers and checking email; it doesn't work. We have a Community Assistance Unit for the Mayor's Office who goes to certain community meetings (which is half the battle, at least they can hear what's going on), but they do not report back to the other agencies; none of it works. We do not know how to talk to each other. We do not have a built-in process that works for any regular successful engagement where people feel heard, and I don't know of a government that does. Why is government so

Amy Chester

Project Manager and later Managing Director of Rebuild by Design scared to talk to the community? A lot of individuals in government had to be elected, so you'd think they would be accustomed to talking to their constituents, but for some reason, when they become part of government, they become scared of criticism and shy away from having open conversations. For a lot of community members, they really are only looking to be heard. With the Rebuild by Design competition, we forced the design teams to go into the communities to work with the people who were most affected by the storm. We encouraged the teams to share their ideas with communities, ask for feedback, incorporate that feedback, and then go back to the community to show them how the designs changed. This process showed communities that their opinions actually mattered, because they did to us. And after the presentation of the design opportunities, the projects really started to change to reflect the feedback the design teams were hearing from the communities. And then we saw that the designers were going back to do even more meetings, so they must have been getting feedback that was very useful. This process would give us the stakeholder support we knew we needed for implementation. In the end, there was this level of continuous interest, energy and excitement, talking to this person and that one, getting them on board, hearing their feedback. It became really exciting, because the process we created was working for everyone."

comes with no one having exclusive ownership, and that is a great strength. Rebuild by Design is not the federal government, it is not the community, it is not an NGO, neither private sector nor philanthropy. Rebuild by Design is all of these, at the crossroads of all stakeholders, all intentions and all ambitions. It is a new commons. This positions us to consider things from all sides and allows us to operate with maximum flexibility as a team. Most of all, it gives everyone the opportunity to join in, to discover that if you are willing to put your cards on the table, join forces and invest in the partnership, you can really have an impact. Not by power, but by knowledge, by expertise and by commitment.

85%
OF THE REGIONAL HISTORIC WETLANDS HAS BEEN DEVELOPED OR LOST

2.5
MILLION INHABITANTS IN THE NEW YORK & NEW JERSEY METROPOLITAN AREA LIVE IN THE FLOOD ZONE

66%
OF THE MOST VULNERABLE COMMUNITIES LIVE WITHIN A 1/2 MILE OF THE FLOOD ZONE

80%
OF THE REGIONAL FUEL STORAGE IS IN THE FLOOD ZONE

75%
OF THE NET ANNUAL POWER GENERATION IS IN THE 100 YEAR FLOOD ZONE

The analysis of the MIT CAU + ZUS + URBANISTEN team shows infrastructural, environmental, and social vulnerabilities.

Unexpectedly Official

The White House calls—they want to use our regional analysis when granting the second tranche of federal funding for disaster recovery. I'm delighted by the request, but we're not ready for it. From the beginning of the research phase, our plan has been that the Institute for Public Knowledge will integrate the different teams' analyses into a single regional study, but that study is far from complete. We know the region pretty well now—its protection levels, its governance and policies, its environmental, social and economic vulnerabilities. Such an analysis will be important in many ways. It is a window into what is actually going on, a portrait of a region's interconnections and vulnerabilities. It facilitates the identification of opportunities at all scales and smart interventions.

In such a complex and diverse region as New York and New Jersey, our factual analysis will be a tool that shows opportunities and allows good decisions to be made without requiring a new (normative) regional policy or strategy on which we must agree. If we don't have to agree on a new policy or strategy—which is always difficult—we are better positioned to get things done. The analysis provides a common, factual baseline for how things actually are. It is a tool by which interventions can be evaluated.

Ideally, the White House or anyone else would be able to use the IPK report to see what we know, sorting by theme and by location—the Rockaways, for example, or the impact of green infrastructure. Right now, we are a long way from achieving that level of accessibility and integration in our findings, but we can't turn the White House down. If the grantees use our analysis as part of their action plans, which describe how they will invest federal funds, then that helps align their plans with what we have done and integrates the work of Rebuild by Design into the operations of government. This will be a small step in the culture change we hope to bring about. So with IPK in the lead, we speed up our work and are able to send the report in time. When the second tranche of HUD's Sandy relief funds are distributed, Rebuild by Design's research is mentioned as a reference for the grantees' action plans.

This Is Our Money

The day before the first anniversary of Hurricane Sandy, October 28, the teams make their first public presentation at the NYU campus on Washington Square Park. Each team presents their share of the research and three to five project opportunities they have identified. So many people want to attend that the fire marshal has barred the door after 700, leaving many citizens waiting on the sidewalk. It feels surreal to see this kind of interest. That evening, we repeat the presentation in New Jersey to another full house, over 250 people. Everyone can see the writing on the wall: Rebuild by Design is for real. There is a political message embedded in the huge crowds that come to see the work, a message for the mayors and governors and even for Shaun Donovan: Don't ignore this. Don't ignore us.

According to government theory, the federal government is not supposed to get involved in local and regional politics. So much for that—there is theory, and there is practice, and what we have done in practice is deeply involve the feds by creating a region-wide collaboration. Now we see the provisional results: forty-one proposals, midwifed by the federal government. For all intents and purposes, federal officials will tell the affected cities and states which of these they will

The first public presentation, one year after Hurricane Sandy

"The comprehensive approach is crucial to protect our cities for the future and to adapt to the impact of climate change. And Rebuild by Design was the first time for the federal government to take on this comprehensive approach. So I jumped on right away and worked as hard as I could with the team to ultimately be one of the winners."

build. That's not how a federal system is supposed to work. Normally, the feds provide the funding and the states and cities—the grantees—determine how to spend it. It's the sort of thing that's just not done, but we're doing it. This is why collaboration has been so essential from the beginning. "No other federal system in the world could handle anything like this," observes Junaid Ahmad, Senior Director of the World Bank's Global Water Practice. "We should bring this to the world. We could all benefit from this approach."

Now the political leaders and staffs of those grantees understand that the decisions we make at this stage in the competition will determine what they build, and they resist. "This is our money," they say. Counterweighting that political pressure are the partners who see Rebuild by Design not as a threat but an opportunity. They are here to see their interests safeguarded, to urge us to pick their neighborhood, their city.

We begin the process of winnowing the forty-one proposals down to ten. They range in scope from small-scale coastal projects to large-scale infrastructure, from a policy intervention tied to a communications strategy, to investments in roads, buildings and networks, to building with nature. We consider not only their technical merits, but their power to address regional and local needs, the geographical spread, and the range of project types. We think about who will support them, who will be able to get them done. This is a deeply political set of decisions, and Shaun stays in close touch with New York Governor Andrew Cuomo, New Jersey Governor Chris Christie, and both Mayor Bloomberg of New York and his newly-elected successor Bill de Blasio. We remind ourselves that we cannot negotiate down if we want to make a difference. Every conversation with the teams, communities, federal agencies and grantees is about being ambitious. We cannot end up with a mediocre plan simply because that's what we negotiated.

We lose some real beauties, among them SCAPE's impressive proposal in Jamaica Bay. We embrace complexity, but the spaghetti-like complexity of the bay and its many, misaligned players—the Port Authority, the city, the states, the federal government—is too much for a project that must be ready for implementation in a year. Rebuild by Design is not an ideas competition; implementation must be within reach We take SCAPE's Jamaica Bay proposal outside the competition and insert it in the separate development process. The analysis and approach are inspirational and solid and shouldn't be wasted. (They aren't—the U.S. Army Corps of Engineers later incorporates SCAPE's work into a comprehensive plan for Jamaica Bay.) For the next stage of the competition, SCAPE will focus on an inspiring, transformative project for Staten Island.

On November 10, Donovan calls me with his list of ten. Then he checks with Governor Christie and gets the thumbs up. On November 14, we make public ten specific

"For me, Rebuild by Design was a process that enabled our firm to apply at 1:1 what we had already been intensively working on, frankly. We had been advancing research about the New York region, sea-level rise, climate change and habitat loss in a number of different ways. We had done a mapping project on Jamaica Bay and looked at how it changed over time. I'd written an essay and co-edited a book about rethinking Jamaica Bay as ecological infrastructure. On the invitation of the Museum of Modern Art, we did a project called Oyster-tecture and developed some of the ideas about resilience strategies for bays and marshlands. So when the call for Rebuild by Design proposals came in, I had a pretty clearly-defined sense of what I thought needed to be done and what our role could be. We had done years' worth of research, and for me, Rebuild by Design was a means of implementing ideas. In that sense, I was also wary of the competition aspect of it. It can be very exciting for policy makers and others as a sort of jump-starter of conversation and dialogue, but often it stays just a proliferation of images

Kate Orff

Founder and Partner of SCAPE

and it's not rigorous or followed through on. But for me, the added value of Rebuild by Design was this very, very sharp and clear justification for matching the strategy with specific sites. So we looked at Barnegat Bay, we looked at the bays in New Jersey, we looked at Jamaica Bay. And we looked at Raritan Bay, which is where the Living Breakwaters project was ultimately developed. This was incredibly helpful, because what we had not had the ability to do before Rebuild by Design, was to actually fund a process and a methodology. And here, we had time and space to focus on and advance this set of ideas about ecological infrastructure, which all the time had been done in the spaces between other projects. So we developed the whole mapping system that layered up ecological strategies with specific places, so we had a very clear and consistent site selection framework that came out of that process."

opportunities spread across the region, each with the potential to grow into a real project. We are ready to move into the final stage of the competition. We must firm up local coalitions to design with us the best possible solutions for each of these ten places. In a few months, Shaun will determine which of these to fund. First, though, they have to be designed.

→ One City Parade in Asbury Park, New Jersey

DANIEL PITTMAN–"Our project in Hoboken was no real design product. It wasn't a place or a thing, it was a strategy–a framing with a handful of keywords to hold an entire approach to resiliency for the city and a way in which to communicate that effectively. And regardless of how the actual project is being implemented, the city has already adopted that framework. That was what we were selling."

Daniel Pittman

Business Manager - Strategy/Innovation at OMA from 2012 to 2016

JELTE BOEIJENGA What for you—as a designer—stands out in the process of Rebuild by Design?

DANIEL PITTMAN It was unique, and different from any other competition. Firstly, given the expectation of what a competition is and the competing part of it, I remember you had all these teams and suddenly we're told to collaborate and do research together. What? If we're in competition, are we giving up our strategic advantage? So that was a very different kind of framing from the outset. But what was interesting was that it wasn't done in isolation: there was an entire process and education associated with the call. Usually in competitions there might be a level of introduction into the problem, but then you go out and do it yourself. But here in the research phase we had field trips and meetings with people, all of these experts and a whole array of resources to educate the teams. And I would say that was probably a core piece of the Rebuild by Design competition.

> **"It was clear that these designers were access to resources and a potential."**

Secondly I think what was very unique was the position that we were put in as designers, basically being the gateway for a very large amount of money. Because as a designer, you're usually the one that's begging for money to do this great idea. Rarely are you the one that has the resources behind you and you suggest where it might go. That's a gross simplification, given the politics, given all of the things that were needed to demonstrate and unlock the money, but it was clear that these designers were access to resources and a potential.

JB If you look at the final plan of the competition phase, could you describe to what extent or in what way this plan was really influenced by this process?

DP Firstly, there was a clear set of requirements that are beyond what you would typically expect of a design competition: cost-benefit analysis, engaging in conversations with all the experts, demonstration of stakeholder support and buy-in, the implementation strategy, next to the design and selling that. So the result was something that was typically far more than we would ever do as designers. It was putting us as a part of conversations that we would otherwise not participate in. Because usually no one trusts a designer with anything that smacks of money.

One consequence in particular came from the heavy emphasis on the stakeholder engagement—because again, the scale of the effort was far beyond what we would typically do—which meant that you're spending time reaching out and communicating to various stakeholders, and not developing design ideas. The competition is rebuild by *design*, but I would argue that actually if you look across the whole, design in the conventional design competition sense wasn't really what was happening. It was more design *thinking*. So we were very shallow in terms of developing interpretative design ideas; it was more about developing a process that had a robust kind of logic to it. To take our project in Hoboken, I would argue that there was no real design product. It wasn't a place or a thing, it was a strategy–a framing with a handful of keywords to hold an entire approach to resiliency for the city and a way in which to communicate that effectively. And regardless of how the actual project is being implemented, the city has already adopted that framework in the way they talk about all of their other stuff. So that was a piece that we were selling.

> **"Without examples to build on, you're always selling the idea and the potential of something rather than 'here's the evidence, it worked once so we can do it again.'"**

I would argue that the greatest innovation is the competition itself, rather than anything that was generated because of it. Especially given the state of American politics. What was intriguing was engaging with that level of complexity–the vertical of government and the horizontal of how society works, and understanding how you could reconcile those in design. Because certainly designers are *yielded* towards integrating different thinking, but being able to play that out in such a deliberate matter where you have the expert in sociology there in the room, you have the climate scientists, et cetera, was really unique.

In many ways the built product for me is down the road and less interesting than the result of the conversation and changing the nature of the way we look at things. That's my view of the success. But of course that's always easy. You do need to build things, you need that evidence in order to support that. Because without the precedent or the case study, examples to build on, you're always selling the idea and the potential of something rather than "here's the evidence, it worked once so we can do it again."

JB Does it also mean that you're not disappointed that the project is developing in different directions compared to the final design of the competition phase, because it's not about this alignment here or there?

DP I would say that I completely agree with that sentiment. For me it was always about the framing rather than a particular design. All of the imagery that we did during the competition was interesting, but it was suggestive. All the permitting and the approvals were yet to come. So if anything, part of the success was being able to sell an idea whilst not having anything concrete behind that idea. And what is happening during feasibility is a translation from the vision and what is possible, to how to actually put it on the ground with all the consequences. Ultimately, this was a competition and a lot of the success has to do with how loud and iconic or how strong your soundbites were. So it's about salesmanship and making things sexy and less about developing innovative ideas. Which is what competitions in many ways are about, kind of bringing light onto an idea. Which is good, but if it's all about creating noise and excitement there's also a danger that if you don't deliver against that, you run the risk of creating disappointment and to a degree a level almost of resentment. Big singing things, but actually we're not creating.

"The greatest innovation is the competition itself, rather than anything that was generated because of it."

JB   Because the focus on selling and finding stakeholders is so dominant, you also might run the risk of having sold an idea which might not have been strong enough to really deliver quality in the long run?

DP   Exactly. Because you can identify all of the important issues, like how has it to do with historic preservation, or environmental impact, cost-benefit ratio, whatever. That's easy. But figuring out what the criteria for assessment are, what is the relative weighting, then it becomes difficult. Because to a degree that's not empirical, there's an element of judgment and political considerations in terms of "Oh, actually in this community it's all about preserving green, in this community it's…" et cetera. The reason why I raise this particularly is because with this type of project, you're dealing with a political context and you need to be able to operate within that. Having the two work together is difficult. You're trying to reconcile what is the ideal circumstance with the political reality.

▲

MARC FERZAN, TERRENCE BRODY, VINCENT MEKLES–"Rebuild by Design was touted to us as an opportunity with a funding solution. There's a lot of talent in the world–architects, designers, planners, engineers who can develop really thoughtful solutions. From our vantage point you can't get things done unless you can get them funded. So all the best plans won't yield results unless funding solutions can be identified."

Marc Ferzan

Terrence Brody

Vincent Mekles

Executive and Deputy Executive Directors of the New Jersey Governor's Office of Recovery and Rebuilding from 2012 to 2016

JELTE BOEIJENGA   The three of you were part of the New Jersey Governor's Office of Recovering and Rebuilding after Hurricane Sandy. What was your perspective on Rebuild by Design from this position?

MARC FERZAN   I think the biggest challenge for us was that something as innovative and interesting as a design competition was being suggested and administered in the aftermath of a multi-billion dollar disaster. It was at a time when there were many initiatives that were ongoing to clean up and address pressing and immediate challenges. For us, representing the interests of New Jersey, we had to approach disaster recovery in expedient ways to get the job done and solve countless immediate problems, but we also wanted to incorporate as much innovation and opportunity to build back better and stronger with resilient strategies in mind. Perhaps most challenging was that all of our resources were already spread so thinly on managing the crisis when the design competition came to bear. So bringing in the best minds from around the world to tackle problems, great idea. Trying to manage that process in the midst of emerging from chaos added layers of challenge. So, one component I would recommend for future design competitions is to avoid implementing them in the aftermath of a disaster.

VINCENT MEKLES   One of the challenges for government is that the money often seems to follow the bad events. Getting money to do things proactively and getting people to focus proactively is much more of a challenge. It's hard to get people to focus outside of a disaster context. The idea behind Rebuild by Design is absolutely the right one, being proactive, being thoughtful, protecting assets before those assets are destroyed, because rebuilding them and then protecting them always costs multiples of what it costs to protect them in the first place.

"Money often seems to follow the bad events. Getting money to do things proactively is much more of a challenge."

We need regional integrated infrastructure solutions and we need those implemented before the disaster happens. So the policy behind Rebuild by Design is absolutely on point. I think the timing of the implementation presented a lot of significant challenges. Because it's not just about an infrastructure project for flood protection, it's also about how we're going to get the state, municipal and county governments to work together, it's about identifying in advance all the different regulatory hurdles you're likely to run into. You need to see that entire playing field and you need the time to actually digest all of those issues. Time, quite frankly, the Rebuild by Design teams didn't have, just because it was right after a disaster and this money needed to get obligated, and to get obligated you needed to work back from essentially a 2017 deadline, so they basically had six months to come up with the project. So time as much as anything else is critical to getting these projects running.

JB Despite its limitations, and the struggle perhaps, New Jersey State eventually embraced the competition. What were the positives for you?

MF Rebuild by Design was touted to us as an opportunity with a funding solution. There's a lot of talent in the world—architects, designers, planners, engineers who can develop really thoughtful solutions. From our vantage point, having worked in government, you can't get things done unless you can get them funded. So all the best plans won't yield results unless funding solutions can be identified. The two Rebuild by Design projects that ultimately were successful on the New Jersey side of the river also involved communities and regions that faced repetitive flooding, beyond from just Hurricane Sandy. So, the potential of being able to come up with solutions for regions in New Jersey with chronic flooding challenges, that was something that really appealed to us. And we recognized that we were getting some very talented perspectives on potential design solutions.

And we were able to essentially leverage the hard work we had been undertaking relative to analysis throughout the state, while relying on expertise within our state departments and agencies, across environmental challenges, across different sectors, housing, infrastructure, economic impacts and resilience, et cetera.

TERRENCE BRODY By the time Rebuild by Design officially kicked off we had a pretty developed blueprint for our comprehensive rebuilding strategy for New Jersey. So I think we saw Rebuild by Design complementing that and potentially bringing additional funding to help. We were very focused on regional solutions to address, because it really was a statewide event. It wasn't an event that just hit one or two towns. So we were very focused on regional solutions and we saw Rebuild by Design as an opportunity to help realize additional regional solutions, both financially and by bringing additional capacity to the State. The two projects that got funded, the Hudson River and the Meadowlands project, those were both areas that got severely impacted during Sandy and were very much on our radar.

"We were very focused on regional solutions to address, because it really was a statewide event."

And we already had previously engaged some of our top universities in the state to really look at how Sandy impacted, where the vulnerabilities are and what are some proposed solutions to mitigate the risk of flooding in the future. So we were able to download that information and once these projects got funding we were able to build out capacity within the Department of Environmental Protection, New Jersey Transit and some other state agencies, to really focus on moving these projects forward.

JB At a certain moment it became clear that CDBG-DR funds would be used for the Rebuild by Design projects, money over which–under other circum-stances–the grantees would have had more control. How did you deal with the challenges this presented on the political level?

MF At the time that the concept of Rebuild by Design was made public, it was not clear to us, and similarly, it was not clear to our federal government counterparts either, how much money in total would come to New Jersey through the various disaster recovery funding streams, including the HUD CDBG-DR funds. If your question is: was there stress for us relative to the broad needs throughout the State that we had identified and for which funding solutions were needed, separate and apart from the Rebuild by Design projects? Yes, there certainly was. Even though Rebuild by Design was a priority, we knew

the projects were going to get done and we were very optimistic that they could be impactful and meaningful; we were also very aware of the multiple billions in broader needs we had identified throughout the State, and we reflected those needs in our applications for CDBG-DR allocations to HUD, and elsewhere. So, our analysis was out there for the public to see. While the Rebuild by Design projects presented great potential for us, there was a lot of stress relative to all the other fundamentals that we wanted to address.

VM At the time it became announced, even before we knew that the CDBG-DR funding was going to be used, we still didn't know, nor did our federal counterparts, whether we would have enough money to serve all the people in our housing rebuilding program or in our rental programs. So it's difficult to develop broad support from the public when you have to say, well I don't know if I'm going to have money to rebuild this person's home that was destroyed, but I'm going to do this huge, cool innovative project of hundreds of millions of dollars.

"We still didn't know whether we would have enough money to serve all the people in our housing rebuilding program. "

MF   Yes. Having a very aggressive and clear public relations campaign is just as important as managing governance structures or regulatory challenges. Because at the end of the day, many of these decisions are being made by public figures who should necessarily seek public buy in. Accountability to the public has to be part of the equation. Helping to put things in context in ways that are accessible and clear to the public, reflecting benefits and limitations, really increases the chances that any plans can actually be realized. Remember, at the time we were coming out of the disaster, tremendous need had been identified, there was widespread devastation throughout the state, and a design competition was announced with the caveat that not everyone was going to win.

> "It was a time when the people were really hurting, they were frustrated, and they were still trying to put their lives back together."

That creates tension for public messaging for many reasons, but certainly more so because this wasn't just an ordinary time for government to evaluate opportunities. It was a time when the people were really hurting, they were frustrated, and they were still trying to put their lives back together. So, when I talk about an aggressive public messaging campaign, those are the fundamentals: making sure that the administrators of the competition are really putting themselves in the shoes of the public relative to what's going to be most important to constituents, what their questions are likely to be. And the more answers that can be addressed, I think that's what fuels engagement. That's what gives people reassurance that proposed solutions are going to yield good results, and therefore they can get behind them and give them their support.

VM   The Rebuild by Design team just didn't have time to design fully designed, feasible projects. So they gave really great conceptual ideas. They were fantastic in moving the ball forward, but even with high-level concepts we still can't fully engage the public until the feasibility studies are completed. So when we got a question like: will this project involve the filling of wetlands? Well the truth is, we don't know, because until there's a feasibility study completed and we have taken five alternatives down to three, including a no-build alternative, until we've analyzed everything, the project and the price, it's only then that you can sit down with the public and have an informed conversation. They can at that point make up their mind with full information as to whether or not they support it.

TB   A related point is managing the expectations for your stakeholders. A lot of folks were under the misimpression that the design teams were handing over to us completed construction drawings and that the shovel was going to be in the ground immediately. As we all know, that's far from the truth. That was really just a first step in a pretty protracted process. Socializing the public to that process early on, showing residents that they're not going to be out of the mandate to get flood insurance next year, is important. I think people thought that was going to happen fairly immediately. And it may never happen. So really managing expectations is an important feature, otherwise you lose people at a certain point.

JB To what extent were the Rebuild by Design projects perceived as part of a regional approach? And to what extent did this scale and scope help or not help in the political process?

TB When you look at the Hudson River project, if that would have been just a Hoboken project, they would have built walls, separating them from Weehawken. That could either not help Weehawken with their flooding or potentially be a disaster. But instead the project took a much more regional approach. If we create berm systems around Weehawken Cove, we're going to prevent the surge from coming down into Hoboken, but also to Weehawken. So from a regional standpoint it might not really be broad based, but it's definitely a regional way of thinking and helping more than one jurisdiction. I think the

Meadowlands is an even better example, where it's helping a much broader geographical area, helping more jurisdictions, more local governments. Right now it's been scaled based on available funding—there's a pilot that's primarily going to help two municipalities in particular with some benefits to adjacent municipalities—but the whole master plan is a much broader regional plan. It needs significant funding to be realized but it's absolutely on a regional basis.

> "When you're trying to get beyond crises with limited funding, you learn quickly that all needs won't be met."

MF We recognized scalability. You always have to think about scale relative to available funds. We had an expression that we used across so many different projects in New Jersey in the aftermath of Hurricane Sandy, that success breeds success. Relative to Meadowlands or the Hudson River project, we recognized that there probably wouldn't be full funding to realize the full scope of either project. But if we maintained a regional perspective, and things could be designed in ways to tackle the bigger problems and then scale things back to generate success piecemeal, we felt that that would be lasting and that that would in and of itself build momentum for expansion on that scale.

When you're trying to get beyond crises with limited funding, you learn quickly that all needs won't be met. And therefore, when you're in government, you have to manage expectations with the public. We felt strongly that regional solutions could be something that the public would understand and embrace, perhaps even more so than fixing one particular thing in an impacted community, however innovative the solution might be. Such a regional perspective enables government to reassure constituents that leadership is seeking to tackle the broader challenges in ways to ultimately benefit wider cross-sections of the population. It also explains why, with limited funding, projects may need to start more narrowly, but can be extended over time according to a well thought through and cohesive plan.

JB What are the lessons learned from Rebuild by Design and the efforts you made in the aftermath of Sandy? What kind of institutional change is necessary?

MF I think the very nature of complicated projects means that you need broad and varied stakeholder support. Very often meaningful projects can span multiple municipalities, so you need support from corresponding leadership. You also need support from individual constituents and businesses, key special interest groups, and state and federal government agencies.
And without ongoing focus and support from these various stakeholders, it can be difficult to look at necessary larger-scale projects and think about how government can do good for the public in confronting the more significant challenges. One of the things that proved to be critical in New Jersey following Hurricane Sandy is that we centralized the approach to problem solving. When Governor Christie created the Office of Recovery and Rebuilding, he established one team to coordinate all of these different players at the local, state, and federal levels across the public and private sectors to champion recovery and rebuilding projects. And this institutional professional focus in government needs to be empowered. Relative to New Jersey, I expect the experience following Hurricane Sandy will forever change the focus of future administrations. A lot of fundamental perspective and professional support and technology was embedded into the state departments and agencies, and that will hopefully transcend administrations. But I would love to see more of an ongoing effort in New Jersey, in New York, and around the country, to focus on resilience and making sure that ongoing coordination remains a priority.

"The experience following Hurricane Sandy will forever change the focus of future administrations."

Because otherwise it will continue to be very difficult to get critical projects done. Without having assigned individuals who champion those projects and coordinate all of the different stakeholders to ensure that issues are being evaluated and decisions are being made, progress will be delayed.

> "That culture of rebuilding with resilience was a necessary by-product of recovering from Sandy. The challenge will be how to keep that focus once the disaster's rebuilding is largely over."

VM   Immediately following Sandy there was a focus on not just building back, but building back stronger and more resilient. And we tried to incorporate that into all of our different initiatives and all of our different funding sources, whether it's buying out properties in flood-prone areas or elevating residences. So I think that culture of rebuilding with resilience was a necessary by-product of recovering from Sandy. The challenge will be how to keep that focus once the disaster's rebuilding is largely over. Because it's easy to then settle back into old, reactive ways. So how do you keep that focus, say in wartime and peacetime. How do you keep that focus on resilience in peacetime? You have it in the recovery, how do you

keep it going forward? I think just the length of Rebuild by Design in terms of building will help with that, because the project's going to take time to implement. And so that will keep that cultural focus on resilience going forward.

▲

DAWN ZIMMER–"People want to know that we're hearing out their concerns and that we're trying to address them. It's a process for people to understand and we help them to understand and show them that this is not something to be afraid of, but something that can really benefit our community in many different ways."

Dawn Zimmer

Mayor of Hoboken from 2009 to 2017

JELTE BOEIJENGA   What opportunity did Rebuild by Design present for you?

DAWN ZIMMER   I saw Rebuild by Design as a tremendous opportunity for Hoboken. In the United States we're not used to taking a comprehensive approach to the flooding problem. We tend to take a very individual approach: how are you going to individually protect your home? That doesn't work in the city environment. In my perspective, cities have to take the comprehensive approach. It's crucial to protect our cities for the future and to adapt to the impact of climate change. And Rebuild by Design was the first time for the federal government to take on this comprehensive approach. So I tell my residents it is a tremendous opportunity. Before, when we were trying to get support from FEMA or from the State, the answer was always "We can fund– for example–your fire station, we can help you to protect that." But if my fire station doesn't flood but I can't get to it, it's useless. To a certain extent, that approach is almost a waste of federal dollars. We as a country are spending so much money on being reactive and not spending the money cost-effectively. So I saw Rebuild by Design as an opportunity to be part of a completely innovative approach and jumped on right away and worked as hard as I could with the team to ultimately be one of the winners.

Hoboken has been taking different actions to try and address our flooding from storm surge, but it was the Rebuild by Design process that helped us connect everything–the planning, the connection with our next-door neighbor Weehawken–and recognize that it would be kind of silly for each of us to build something along each of our borders. We should do something that connects, and use the cove that connects Weehawken and Hoboken. And we should build it in a way that it's a benefit to the entire community and protects Weehawken, Hoboken but also our shared critical assets of the North Hudson Sewage Authority. Rebuild by Design greatly changed the realm of the possible for us. There weren't limits based on arbitrary municipal boundaries anymore. It was really, what's the best project to reduce flood risk in an area that has the greatest value?

> "We as a country are spending so much money on being reactive and not spending the money cost-effectively."

Rebuild by Design was really taking a chance, because it was saying: okay, we're going to go through this process and we're going to work collaboratively and it's going to be a process. And it has taken longer to get to where we need to go to, but at the end of the day it's going to be money well spent. Especially for Hoboken, if we're hit by another Sandy, which we eventually will be, that's all we need to be in the black. The investment will pay itself back with one major storm.

JB What stands out in this process?

DZ I think that the collaborative approach is extremely important and that out of that approach you get the best product. For the first time I think ever, three levels of government worked so effectively together. Rebuild by Design almost forced everyone to work collaboratively, with the professionals, knowing that the funding is there, to get the project done and designed well. We were meeting on a regular basis with the design team, we were talking, rolling up our sleeves, having community meetings and working collaboratively towards that goal.

What I've gotten out of this process is the importance of the design, looking at things from every angle, getting the expertise from so many different kinds of professionals and taking the community's concerns into consideration. We know that we're doing things in a way that meets their concerns. It is because of the design process, because of the collaborative approach, because we've got the State working with us and we know what permits we need, because the federal agencies are giving their input. It really is the policy, the design, the engineering, it's the community engagement, it's the overlap of a lot of different things that makes it work. Because at the end of the day if you don't have all the

players working together, you're not going to get it done.

And yes, it's a slower process but it is ultimately, in the long run, a faster process. You don't want to get to the end and find out nobody wants it or that there are huge permitting issues and you can't do it. So we're taking it step by step by step. With this progressive approach, looking at things from all angles along the way, you end up being able to get across the finish line. Whereas if you just race across, you might just trip and break your leg and be done.

JB Right now, you're in the process of implementation. What are your biggest concerns now?

DZ I think the biggest challenge is to make sure that a collaborative and innovative approach continues all the way through the process. It has been a real challenge, and it's an ongoing challenge, to get support from the community, to have the community understand why this is important, and to hear out and try to address their concerns. As much as people are concerned about the impact of climate change, ultimately they're also really concerned about themselves. What does it look like right outside my door? What's it going to look like in my neighborhood? How is it going to affect my neighbor or the waterfront? They want to know that we're not going to have just an ugly wall. And that produces a lot of interest in the project. A couple of people that misunderstand, they create a flyer, next thing you know it just snowballs and you've got some real communications challenges. But nothing comes easy and you've got to keep advocating to make sure that the collaborative approach is there.

Unfortunately in this country there remains a huge misunderstanding. Even in Hoboken, I'm a little bit surprised–even though we were so severely impacted by Sandy, 80% of our city was under water, it was devastating, but it's in the past and people don't remember it as vividly as you might think they do–but there are residents that feel like "well, a hundred-year storm, we just had a hundred-year storm, so that means we won't have anything for another hundred years." But that is not at all the way it works. It's just a percentage of risk. And that percentage is going to increase every year.

> **"You need to find elected leaders who believe in this and who are willing to put themselves out there."**

So we went through a serious process. We've really had to go out and listen, so we understand. We've created a community advisory group, had smaller meetings across the city with different neighborhood groups, which set up for the greater success at the public meeting we held because people were able to go to the meetings better informed, able to ask the right questions and create a deeper level of understanding. And that process will continue. They want to know that we're hearing out their concerns and that we're trying to address them. It's a process for people to understand. And we help them to understand and show them that this is not something to be afraid of, but something that can really benefit our community in many different ways. So I really try to be as connected to my community as possible and understand where they are coming from and hearing out their ideas. But ultimately it's a balancing act, because at the same time you have to keep moving on the design process and then you've got to make decisions, you've got to decide and you've got to get it done. It's a serious balancing act.

And this does overlap with the political. You need to find elected leaders who believe in this and who are willing to put themselves out there. I had some council members who said to me: since this isn't popular, maybe we should pull it all back. I said wait a minute, this is the future of Hoboken we're talking about. We've got to work harder, we've got to roll up our sleeves, we've got to go out there and talk to people. We had a couple of meetings where people were just infuriated and angry. Some elected officials just take that and say well, okay, I've got to worry about the next election and walk away from it. That is politically the easier thing to do. So we need people who are really committed too, who can see that things can change. One day people may be angry, but the next day–when you keep talking to them, educating them and hearing them out– you can change the direction of things. That's the approach that I've tried to take, but I've also had council members that didn't want to support me. Some of the reservations we hear from them are the same as the ones we hear from the residents. So it's an education process for them as well.

JB   To what extent did the design work help in this communications challenge?

DZ   Rebuild by Design gave us the framework with which to do the communications and recognize how important it is, but the design is what's driving all of this. If the design isn't there, the community doesn't feel there's going to be benefits for them and that it's not going to destroy the fabric of our city. They need to know and need to be assured that it's a benefit. And as we move towards finalizing what a possible comprehensive plan can be, and we need to get into a little bit more detail, again there's a fear of the unknown. If there isn't some more detail on what it could look like and how it will impact them, then it's hard to get consensus.

When we went back to our core communications, the two points were: the risk is real and a wall is not a wall. Those were the two things. Because the reaction

to the content we released was you're going to build walls in our city. So the design team thought outside of the box to give us examples of how a wall could not be a wall. We're still going through that process and the things that we've seen so far, the public has seen it for some of the first occasions, it's incredible, it's world-class work.

The challenge we've had with communications is that you assemble a team of world-class engineers and architects and you go through a public process, where by producing images and graphics of what the project could be you create this gigantic expectation of the possible. There's this incredible buildup, there's a tenseness. Show me what it's going to look like, I want to see what it's going to be. And then, when you begin the federal process for an environmental impact statement and a feasibility report, and get more into detail of what's going to be the cost-benefit analysis, you almost go back and start from the beginning again. That's a rigorous process, a legal process, an engineering process. And you also find out that some of the designs that were created are not going to be something we can afford to do.

JB   To what extent did the community actually influence the plan for Hoboken?

DZ   We want to do something that is designed well, that can be supported by the community and that we're actually able to implement. We're in the process right now when we're down to three different possible alignments and we're choosing our final alignment. And I think it's because of the process that we're able to get there. And ultimately it's going in different directions than I would have expected. I did expect that we would do something all along the waterfront; I did not expect that there would be so much consensus from the community for an inland alignment. There's huge sensitivity for touching and changing our waterfront. So I think ultimately we'll choose a combination of waterfront and inland alignment, in order to get consensus, get buy-in, have the people see this is something that can be a community benefit. This means we'll be protecting the majority of the city but not quite everyone. It's not the direction I expected, but this can be supported by the community, fits in with the urban landscape and is within the cost constraints that we have. So I think it's a great direction and I think it can be great for Hoboken. I think the vision is important and I think the design is important, but I also think that getting it done is extremely important. You have to do what you can do, but you shouldn't let the perfect get in the way of the good.

"The risk is real and a wall is not a wall."

JB   Could you reflect on possible differences between your expectations three years ago and the results so far?

DZ   We worked extremely hard with the Rebuild by Design team to win. And we won 230 million dollars, we did it! I didn't realize at the time that that was really the beginning of the process. So there's winning and there's getting it done and rolling up our sleeves. So I'd say we're in the third quarter now to make sure that we complete this. And so I think when we won, I didn't realize exactly how much work it would take to get us over the finish line. There's still a lot of work to get done and I think that now I have a deeper understanding of that and a real commitment and we're working really hard to try and make sure we have the support of the council members and different community organizations and different neighborhood groups and just really trying to make sure, because this is an opportunity that I truly believe we will never have again. Especially to have this opportunity and then for some reason we end up not doing it. I know that we won't be ever given this opportunity again. I am a firm believer: you have to work for an opportunity, which we have and now we need to seize it and get it done. So from when we won to where we are now, I didn't have a true understanding of how much work it would be for my administration. But I'm extremely proud of the team that we have, and we've put in a lot of our resources to make sure we work with the state and with the design team to get consensus and get this done.

▲

171

PART IV
Collaborative Design December 2013— April 2014

"At last, we can start to design!" That is the collective spirit when I meet with the teams in New York on December 20, a week after Shaun has selected the ten projects, one per team. I use this opportunity to convey a critical message: don't design alone! I urge everyone to resist the temptation to retreat to their offices, prepare designs and then show them to their respective communities with the intent of engaging afterwards. Instead, I say, continue the collaborative culture, keep the beehive alive. That means each team, working in a specific region, must find partners and create coalitions within their communities as an integral part of the design process. We need those partners, they need us, and those coalitions don't yet exist. I want the teams to understand that beginning to create them is a critical first step.

As much as everyone realized how badly we had needed to spend time on analysis, now they are eager to start the design process, to develop solutions, and to make things work. They kick into high gear. Each team is working with its own coalition of local partners, leading to meetings almost every day with mayors, interest groups, business representatives. I witness an explosion of engagement, creativity and comprehensive thinking.

So many of the people we had relied upon in the research stage to educate us, to broaden our thinking and deepen our understanding, are people we reach out to again in the design stage. We ask them to become our partners in creation. They will be the beneficiaries of the finished projects, and their expertise and local knowledge, as people living and working in the places where the teams want to build, is essential for success. We want them to do more than observe, comment, and approve—we want them to contribute. Once again, that demands an investment of trust to get to true collaboration.

"With Rebuild by Design, we ran a series of public programs in close collaboration with the design teams, titled Scale it Up. These programs helped build connections between the communities and the design teams in a seemingly light-hearted manner, and they allowed people to open up more easily in the later phases of the design process. It may sound silly at first, but there were marching band parades, youth bike tours, a science fair on Staten Island, and building workshops in the Rockaways. Often in projects like these, community engagement is done with maps and sticky note sessions in dreary community centers. Communities often get disillusioned—especially when they don't see the ideas that they floated come to fruition later in the design and implementation process. At Van Alen Institute, we believe that at the beginning of a public design process, the main thing one should focus on is the building of real trust and future relationships between all potential people involved—from designers and community to government. Through Scale It Up, the many people involved in the

David
van der Leer

Executive Director of
Van Alen Institute

competition realized that it can never be just about making a design: it is about developing long-lasting relationships. The most successful design teams in the competition were often the ones that were able to build up actual trust with each of their community partners through these public programs. Everyone, from designers to these community members, wanted to resolve the serious issues they were facing, and they wanted to collaborate. Scale it Up inspired them to go a little further than they would've usually done in a new collaboration."

This is where they will work:

Hunts Point, The Bronx: PENNDESIGN / OLIN
The Meadowlands, New Jersey: MIT CAU + ZUS + URBANISTEN
Red Hook, Brooklyn; Rockaway Beach, Queens;
Asbury Park, New Jersey: HR&A ADVISORS, INC. WITH COOPER, ROBERTSON & PARTNERS
Union Beach, Asbury Park, Tom's River, New Jersey: SASAKI / RUTGERS / ARUP
Staten Island, New York: SCAPE / LANDSCAPE ARCHITECTURE
Nassau County, Long Island: INTERBORO TEAM
Offshore New York and New Jersey: WXY / WEST 8
Bridgeport, Connecticut: WB UNABRIDGED WITH YALE, ARCADIS
Lower Manhattan: BIG TEAM
Hoboken, New Jersey: OMA

Rebuild by Design fields a team of liaison officers to help the design teams build their local coalitions. In some places things come together quickly: Hoboken's dedicated mayor, Dawn Zimmer, lends her critical support early; in Hunts Point, the community organization The Point steps up (but we know we also need to reach the diffuse and diverse business community); and in Manhattan Good Old Lower East Side comes to the table with clear demands: protect the neighborhood and all its faults in the face of gentrification, prepare the community for climate change events but preserve access to the waterfront. Long Island doesn't have mayors for its towns, but rather county officials who play a different kind of role. We get the

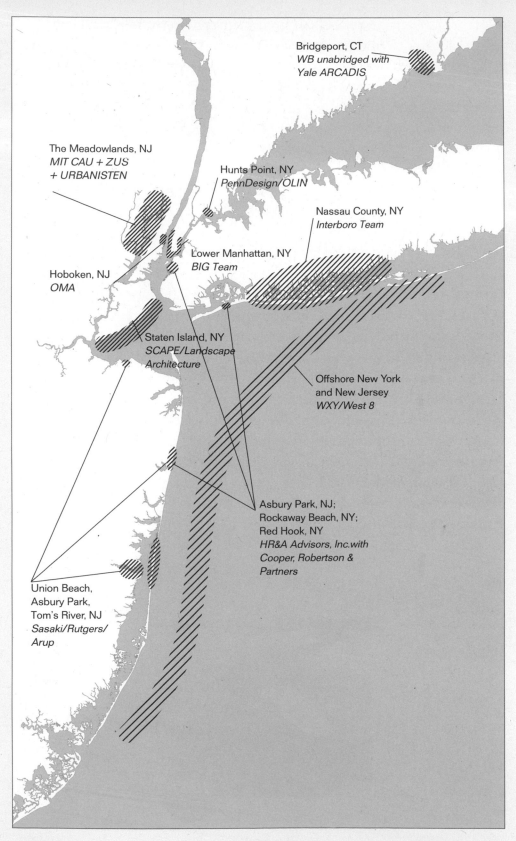

Bridgeport, CT
*WB unabridged with
Yale ARCADIS*

The Meadowlands, NJ
*MIT CAU + ZUS
+ URBANISTEN*

Hunts Point, NY
PennDesign/OLIN

Nassau County, NY
Interboro Team

Lower Manhattan, NY
BIG Team

Hoboken, NJ
OMA

Staten Island, NY
*SCAPE/Landscape
Architecture*

Offshore New York
and New Jersey
WXY/West 8

Asbury Park, NJ;
Rockaway Beach, NY;
Red Hook, NY
*HR&A Advisors, Inc.with
Cooper, Robertson &
Partners*

Union Beach,
Asbury Park,
Tom's River, NJ
*Sasaki/Rutgers/
Arup*

10 Miles

New York Harbor School on board quickly in Staten Island, but it's harder to find partners along the Jersey Shore.

As seems to be true everywhere in the world, professionals in this region don't talk much to nonprofessionals, so I find it gratifying to bring them together under the auspices of the design process and witness the catalyzing effect of collaborating. We're able to tie into regional collectives like Occupy Sandy and to more siloed organizations, too, creating connections that challenge institutional inertia and operational isolation.

Hunts Point, The Bronx, New York City

From day one, the PennDesign / OLIN team has been camped out in Hunts Point in the South Bronx. This is a special place, and not in entirely good ways. It is part of the richest, greatest city in America, yet it is the poorest Congressional District in the United States. At its heart is the Hunts Point Food Distribution Center, the operational core of a network that feeds 22 million people in the New York region and employs more than ten thousand people. It is adjacent to a vulnerable neighborhood challenged by poverty, low pedestrian safety, poor air quality (due to the thousands of daily truck trips, plus associated train traffic to and from the distribution center), and decades of environmental degradation.

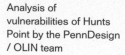

Analysis of vulnerabilities of Hunts Point by the PennDesign / OLIN team

Miraculously, Sandy did not flood Hunts Point, thanks to a fortuitous combination of geographical location, moon, tide and wind. But much of the Food Distribution Center and many related businesses lie in the floodplain, and by 2050, more of this peninsula between the East River and the Bronx River will be vulnerable to flooding from sea level rise. If that happens, New York could find itself without food in as little as two days. This is a place that is both extremely vulnerable in social and environmental terms, and critically important to the entire metropolitan region.

The PennDesign / OLIN team knows their solutions will not be found at the drawing board. They head out to meet everyone they can, asking questions. What makes this neighborhood special? What do its residents value most? How do they experience the wide array of problems? These talks lead to inquiries about how to make the waterfront more accessible to residents. Can space be allocated for storing and discharging storm water runoff? How could we organize truck traffic to decrease environmental impacts and improve the quality of life? It is inherent to the design process that the team consider every need and every vulnerability—water-related, economic, social, environmental. In the process of understanding vulnerabilities and complexities, the team invests both in research and the people who live here, encouraging them to engage the complexity themselves and develop solutions that work toward change and resiliency.

Announcement of the first annual Hunts Point Slam Bake

177

This is not a single community, nor will we create one just by drawing up a plan together. But it does help to throw a party. The PennDesign / OLIN team takes advantage of an event called the Slam Bake, an Iron Chef-inspired cooking contest hosted by Baron Ambrosia, the host of "Bronx Flavor" on the Cooking Channel. The small business community, wholesalers, workers, residents, community groups and youth all come together around their mutual interest in food. While kids show off their skills and businesses explain their objectives, the team presents their analysis and organizes a discussion about a different future for Hunts Point, premised on this idea: we have to take Sandy's near-miss of Hunts Point, and Rebuild by Design's involvement here, to do something truly meaningful. That is what it will take to create a better future and stay here in safety. The Slam Bake provides an opportunity to make and tighten social connections—to find out that Jenny's daughter and Brian's son are at the same school, that Junior shopped at Mary's store for more than a year without ever getting to know her. That social interaction is important for the resilience of Hunts Point and for shaping our project. A comprehensive plan deals with the complexity of the region, and for that, the coalition needs to be comprehensive too, on all counts.

The Meadowlands, New Jersey

The PATH train from Manhattan runs under the Hudson to Secaucus. There, I change to the local. When I emerge into the light, I am disoriented. Manhattan's distant skyline orients me to where I am. The Meadowlands really is another world, a rich ecosystem of wetlands and marshes that in recent decades was widely and poorly urbanized into an industrial landscape dotted with landfills and hazardous industry. Some people call it "the sixth borough," after the five official boroughs that make up New York City (Manhattan, Brooklyn, Bronx, Queens and Staten Island). The Hackensack River leads through the Meadowlands to the Atlantic. During Sandy, it was a conduit for a massive storm surge that overwhelmed the inadequate levees and also flooded the surrounding communities with a toxic brew washed from industrial sites. The storm was a double-whammy to a low-lying region that had already seen its environmental qualities compromised.

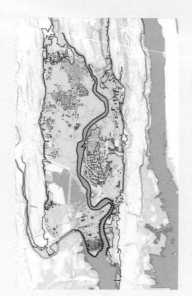 

Analysis of flood risk and protection strategy for the Meadowlands by the MIT CAU, ZUS and URBANISTEN team

MIT CAU, ZUS and URBANISTEN are seeking a holistic solution that will strengthen the damaged ecology of the Meadowlands in ways that protect infrastructure and improve the economy. Their approach includes using the wetlands to soak up excess storm water and concentrating urban development in infrastructure-protected corridors by incentivizing densification and urban renewal. Scale is a challenge here; this region is larger than Manhattan but with a much lower population density spread across multiple towns. There is no way to institute a comprehensive solution at once, and there is risk that uncoordinated efforts won't generate the holistic effects good design can achieve. We have to devise a bite-sized approach that can be instituted over time.

As is the case everywhere, governance and power structures play a key part in establishing a solution. There is a risk of rivalry between cities as they strive to do something to help themselves. Happily, The Meadowlands Commission, appointed by the governor of New Jersey, holds decision-making powers at a regional level. It is counterbalanced by the Meadowlands

Chamber of Commerce, representing the private sector. Starting with these organizations, the team makes the case for a regional and holistic solution, arguing that it is preferable to a scattershot strategy of building walls and levees. Such an approach may take time—it will require mutual understanding and support, but over time it will lower costs and improve resiliency for all.

Asbury Park, New Jersey

When we first came to Asbury Park, we quickly recognized the socio-economic divide that characterized the town and realized that if our approach did not address that divide it would fail. Wealthier residents lived near the ocean. Poorer people grouped inland, across the railroad tracks, in vulnerable, low-lying locations. This division is a source of tension, and that tension had become evident when rebuilding efforts focused on the coast and its famous boardwalk. If we are going to involve the whole community in our approach, we know we have to acknowledge the whole community with its divisions. There will be no single solution, but we need action and a collective event that can bridge the community divide. And we like to celebrate collaboration in part because celebration reveals what is culturally important about a place. The result is a "resilience parade," organized by the Van Alen Institute with the local community, that follows the main road connecting

One City Parade in
Asbury Park

the two sides of town. Our collaborative parade proceeds under the banner "Rebuild One City," for that sense of unity is more important right now than "design."

Two teams work in Asbury Park: HR&A Advisors with Cooper, Robertson & Partners, and Sasaki / Rutgers / Arup. Each team's project is spread across three geographic areas, one of which is in Asbury Park. HR&A focuses on the small business community and identifies two principal areas of concern: physical problems that caused the buildings where small businesses operate to flood, and institutional problems that are limiting business owners' access to relief funds.

During the research phase, HR&A had identified key resiliency problems with the businesses that line the boardwalk and the streets here. They tend to be small, with few financial reserves. They rent spaces that are difficult or impossible to insure, and their landlords are often unresponsive. Their business model depends on tourists, and in the wake of a disaster like Sandy, the absence of tourists can doom many operators who live hand-to-mouth and from season to season. These are precisely the types of businesses that should benefit

"Rebuild by Design had a great impact on me and the work I do at HR&A Advisors. Prior to Rebuild by Design, I (and the firm) worked on efforts to demonstrate and realize the incremental benefits associated with real estate and infrastructure investments every day, but it wasn't standard practice to apply the same principles of these projects to climate adaptation or resilience investments, nor to consider resilience issues when advising on real estate and infrastructure projects. For us, this challenge of resilience was a new problem after Superstorm Sandy, and Rebuild by Design enabled us to experiment with new techniques and methodologies to build a strong approach to resilient planning—one that encompasses physical, economic, community and social resilience. This application of resilience strategy is now pervasive across all the work that we do, whether it relates to 'resilience projects' or not, and it was programs like Rebuild by Design that led us to transform the way we think about city building."

Jamie Springer

Partner at HR&A
Advisors

from emergency relief funds, yet hardly anyone seeks federal loans that are intended for them. Clearly, something is broken in the emergency response.

HR&A works on four levels. The first is the institutional level, to address the broken recovery funding process. Second, the team is working on measures that will benefit states and cities trying to help business owners. The third level is at the scale of individual buildings, assessing why they flooded and developing a technical toolkit that can help prevent flood damage in the first place—low-cost, smart interventions that business owners can deploy to keep the water out and businesses safe. Finally, they investigate interventions for streets, neighborhoods and business-improvement districts that would add resiliency and protection.

While HR&A focuses at the scale of buildings and neighborhoods, Sasaki / Rutgers / Arup analyzes the three coastal

Announcement of
Resilient Red Hook
Open House

typologies that characterize the Jersey Shore: the developed barrier islands, the headlands (where there are boardwalks and dunes), and the inland bay, with marinas and rivers. The team seeks a strategy that fits the development patterns and vulnerabilities of each and can be scaled up and replicated up and down the Eastern Seaboard. How can a culture of risk (such as building on exposed barrier islands) become a culture of living with water, and what are the political, financial and societal roadblocks to, and incentives for, creating that?

Staten Island, New York

I find a package waiting for me in my Washington D.C. office. It contains a T-shirt from the Billion Oyster Project and a handwritten note from a group of eight-year-olds: "Dear Henk— We want the oysters back. Please help us!" Shaun receives a similar gift. These packages embody the SCAPE team's strength. From the beginning, they recognized their shared interests with the New York Harbor School and its Billion Oyster Project. New York Harbor was once host to America's greatest oyster population and fishery, later destroyed by pollution and overharvesting. The project aims to restore the oysters and in so doing clean the harbor and reestablish a key component of its historical ecosystem. Hundreds of children are literally diving into the harbor's waters and what it means for them and their city—learning to swim, observing fish and otherwise immersing themselves in the social, cultural, economic and environmental significance of our waters.

The SCAPE team, which previously had been studying how eco-barriers can provide a community with multiple benefits, including storm surge protection and environmental restoration, immediately saw the Harbor School as a key partner and has returned again and again. SCAPE's plan to build eco-barriers that protect Staten Island from storm surges dovetails with the oyster project and its desire not only to restore the bivalves but to celebrate and strengthen the community's connection to, and understanding of, water and climate change.

CONSTRUCTED REEF
STRUCTURES, REEF
+ SCIENCE PLATFORM

SPAT-ON-SHELL
+ SUBSTRATE
MOUNDS

Cross section of eco-
barriers as breakwaters
by the SCAPE team.

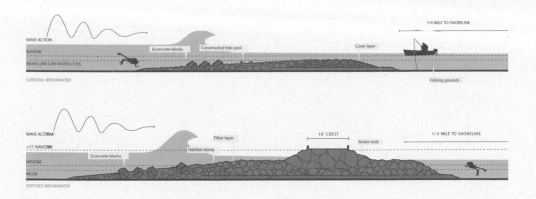

WAVE ACTION

NAVD88
MEAN LOW LOW WATER LEVEL

Econcrete blocks   Constructed tide pool   Cover layer   1/4 MILE TO SHORELINE

SUBTIDAL BREAKWATER   Fishing grounds

WAVE ACTION
+11' NAVD88
NAVD88
MLLW

Econcrete blocks   Habitat stone   Filter layer   16' CREST   Armor rock   1/4 MILE TO SHORELINE

EXPOSED BREAKWATER

↑ Oyster reef, built by members of the community on Staten Island, together with the SCAPE team

SCAPE's other key partner is the U.S. Army Corps of Engineers,
which has jurisdiction over any project to build what are essentially breakwaters. These won't keep water out but will reduce
wave heights and destructive power. The Stevens Institute of
Technology models the designs that will become the center
of SCAPE's proposal. The Corps, charged with defending the
nation, is organized very differently than Rebuild by Design—
it's a military unit with a top-down, hierarchical, rule-bound
structure. The Corps could have resisted what we are doing,
but they do not. U.S. Senator Chuck Schumer Schumer's staff,
who represents New York, enlighten us about the Corps'
stance when we meet to discuss SCAPE's project. This, they
say, will be a great piggyback opportunity for the Corps. This
reminds me of my visit six months earlier to the Washington
D.C. home of Commanding General Thomas Bostick, the
Corps' Chief of Engineers. He had showed me a painting
of Texas, a gift from the spouses of the men he commanded
when his unit deployed to Iraq. That brought home to me
that the mission of the Corps is very much a life-and-death

assignment to protect the United States and its citizens from harm, whether by clearing IEDs from hostile streets or defending coastal communities with dunes and beaches.

This particular project nicely encapsulates the seductive qualities of Rebuild by Design. The Corps is rule-bound, reactive, present in many Congressional districts and dependent on Congress for its funds. It is also part of the American military, able to take good ideas and bring them to scale with, literally, an army of professional staff. The Army is out on the ground, dealing with despair and destruction as it works to put the region back together again, and its leaders understand the need to innovate and do better—even if they are limited by restrictions that they can only invest in "proven technology." In line with Schumer's reasoning, if Rebuild by Design innovates, and our innovations work, the Corps can take those ideas and run with them up and down the coast. The "crazy stuff" we come up with can, if it is successful, become the new standard for the Corps and other federal agencies.

Nassau County, Long Island

Every place we work, we aim for the combination of a comprehensive strategy and actually building a project right away, matching long-term perspective with short-term implementation. When vulnerability is extreme and impacts a whole region, this is a major challenge. Long Island's southern coastline consists of narrow barrier islands, often less than a half a mile across, right up against the Atlantic Ocean. Behind them are bays into which the rivers and creeks flow. Storms bring the threat of water from all sides: the storm surge inundates the barrier islands while the bay overflows, and the rivers have to discharge the rainwater. Much of Nassau County urbanized in the second half of the twentieth century, largely because of its proximity to New York City. Overdevelopment, degraded landscapes, urbanized streams, increased pollution, outdated transit and lack of access to housing and public space led to vulnerable landscapes and communities without the capacity to address the threat of flooding, as Sandy made abundantly clear.

Interconnections within
the natural system of
Long Island by the
Interboro team

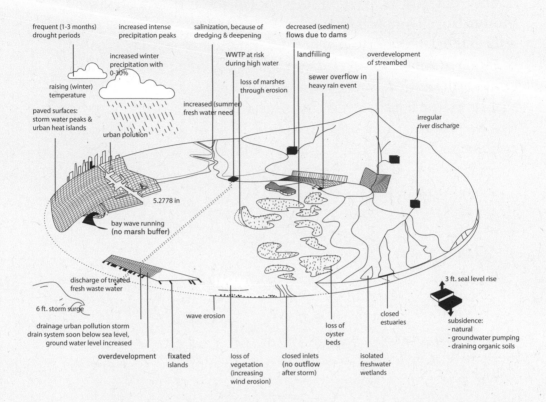

frequent (1-3 months) drought periods

increased intense precipitation peaks

salinization, because of dredging & deepening

decreased (sediment) flows due to dams

increased winter precipitation with 0-30%

WWTP at risk during high water

landfilling

overdevelopment of streambed

raising (winter) temperature

sewer overflow in heavy rain event

loss of marshes through erosion

paved surfaces: storm water peaks & urban heat islands

increased (summer) fresh water need

irregular river discharge

urban pollution

5.2778 in

bay wave running (no marsh buffer)

discharge of treated fresh waste water

3 ft. seal level rise

6 ft. storm surge

drainage urban pollution storm drain system soon below sea level, ground water level increased

wave erosion

closed estuaries

subsidence:
- natural
- groundwater pumping
- draining organic soils

loss of oyster beds

overdevelopment

fixated islands

loss of vegetation (increasing wind erosion)

closed inlets (no outflow after storm)

isolated freshwater wetlands

The Interboro team considers the entire picture, analyzing the system of barrier islands along the Long Island coast, the island's rivers and the way these interact with urban development, beaches, rail, roads and more. How does this function and where did it fail? Where could we intervene, not only to change the system but also to enhance local resilience? What are the opportunities to safeguard the Great South Bay, increase its economic and ecological qualities and give the communities around it the best possible future?

Long Beach is an example of a barrier island that was hit from all sides. During Sandy, ocean waves pounded this Long Island community from the south, while the flooding Mill River raised the bay and backed up streams and inlets. The sewage treatment plant at the mouth of the river was overwhelmed and incapacitated. Now residents of Long Beach want solutions for their particular problems. We come to listen but also to explain: no local solution will stand without a regional approach. The political structure of the island does not include mayors who represent different towns. Instead, county officials are responsible for communities, and they must balance competing pressures from powerful individuals, state and federal politicians, business communities and neighborhood groups. Interboro's regional analysis helps bypass the political maze, and from that approach, local solutions emerge that surprise even the different stakeholders. They understand that we are listening, and this brings buy-in for developing regional resilience through strategic local projects.

TOO BIG for Frag— mentation

The Power of Design

The Power of Design

Complex challenges call for truly comprehensive and inclusive approaches and truly transformative and innovative solutions. We need to unravel the different interdependent demands and connect these in inspiring and sustainable pathways forward. For this approach and these results, we need design: architecture, urban design and landscape architecture. Design is about both process and the outcome. In addressing the impacts of climate change, design is inclusive, seeks synergies, looks ahead and prepares us and our planet for an uncertain future: flexible, adaptive and resilient.

The Power of Design

Design is comprehensive by nature, cutting
across disciplines and silos, uniting rather than
dividing. Once we understand dependencies—how
poverty and health relate to poor infrastructure,
how urbanization touches upon the need for
food, energy and water, ignoring jurisdictional
boundaries—a design approach informs a way
forward that integrates that understanding and
identifies opportunities to solve problems holistically.
Appealing to the imagination but grounded
in analysis, design enables us to sketch new
futures and determine the steps that will get us
there, linking today's conditions with tomorrow's
possibilities. A comprehensive plan consists of real,
innovative projects to implement and inspire others,
kickstarting development and catalyzing change.
A truly integrated design connects social, cultural,
ecological and economic challenges. It connects
regional interdependencies, local needs and
community assets, not by a trade-off of interests—
that is, not by compromising—but by bridging gaps
between quality and safety, between economy,
ecology and society. Integrated solutions add value
across sectors, across scales and through time,
building a sustainable business case.

The Power of Design

This process of design is inherently inclusive. Design challenges the divisions of our daily lives by drawing all interests, all aspects, all questions and all people into a common understanding and a new deal. It invites us all to contribute, to bring our different needs and demands and our unspoken dreams and ideas. By making the envisioned tactile and the ambitious practical, the design approach increases everyone's imaginative capacity and helps us make the future tangible and achievable. In this way, design turns complexity into compelling and inspirational ideas, and translates societal issues into shared ambitions and inspiring narratives about our future. Design helps us tell each other stories about what could be—stories that convince, seduce and make us all believe in them. At this level, design is truly inspirational and aspirational, which makes it political: people who have participated in this process will fight for it and what it promises them. This is why we developed Rebuild "by Design"—to tackle the future and escape the past with vision, by design and in collaboration.

The wxy / West 8 team is the only team working on the full regional scale, across the entire coast of New Jersey and Long Island and beyond. I love their ambition and their scale: early in the research stage, they presented a preliminary business case for building a string of man-made barrier islands nine miles offshore. It is a huge, audacious vision, and it is the kind of solution the entire region needs. These islands would protect New York, New Jersey and Long Island in ways they haven't been protected before, while literally creating new land.

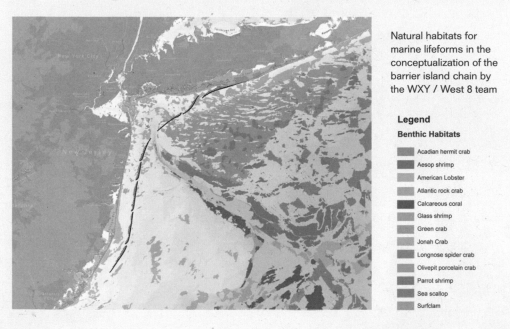

Natural habitats for marine lifeforms in the conceptualization of the barrier island chain by the WXY / West 8 team

Legend
Benthic Habitats

Acadian hermit crab
Aesop shrimp
American Lobster
Atlantic rock crab
Calcareous coral
Glass shrimp
Green crab
Jonah Crab
Longnose spider crab
Olivepit porcelain crab
Parrot shrimp
Sea scallop
Surfclam

Unlike the hard infrastructure (dikes and seawalls) typically constructed as bulwarks against the sea, these islands would not interfere with the cultural, ecological and economic relationships between coastal communities and the ocean.

Of course, what makes this project so appealing is what makes it so challenging: scale. It covers so much ground, literally and metaphorically, involving so many stakeholders, so much money, and so much time. Building these islands could require decades of investment. As exciting as the idea is, many observers consider it too much of a reach, the scale too big, the implementation too far off. I truly believe in the wxy / West 8 vision and urge them to pursue it, because this

regional, large-scale perspective is both important and absent from other proposals. Even if their vision for a chain of barrier islands doesn't come to pass, it's important for us to imagine the idea, research how the project would be done, develop a strategy for doing it and even work on a pilot project to test its capacity.

In the design stage, WXY / West 8 works with Alan Blumberg of the Stevens Institute of Technology to develop models of how the islands would be created and what the effects of building them would be. They want to protect the region while creating new habitat for birds and fish, new recreational spaces, even sites for wind turbines. Their design approach must tackle this regional abstraction to understand the environmental and social impacts of creating what is, in effect, a new world just over the horizon from New York and New Jersey. They bring together experts from the fields of hydrology, economics and even insurance policy to sharpen their analysis and their vision. Whatever they produce will require sustained, long-term effort to implement, but perhaps we can launch a pilot project now.

Bridgeport, Connecticut

Connecticut's largest city, with almost 150,000 residents, lies on the coastline north of Long Island Sound. Despite its size, it is a disadvantaged place. By some measures, it is the poorest city in the state, with 20 percent of the population living under the federal poverty level and unemployment topping 16 percent, more than three times the national average. The main rail line connecting New York City to the Connecticut coast does not stop in Bridgeport, dampening its connection to the economic engine of New York. In Rebuild by Design, Bridgeport Mayor Bill Finch saw opportunity right away. Hurricane Sandy flooded the rocky coast and Housatonic River that runs through the city. Impervious surface and a backlog in infrastructure investments meant that the water stayed, and again, as we discovered throughout the entire region, the poor were the most vulnerable. Finch's city needed help on many fronts.

Bridgeport was in a weak political position. Its finances were strained even before the hurricane hit, it lacked the jurisdictional capacity to scale up any solution, and any Community Development Block Grant Disaster Recovery funds awarded out of the Hurricane Sandy Recovery Bill would be directed to the state, not to coastal cities. Mayor Finch understood right away that Rebuild by Design could help draw attention to Bridgeport and raise state and federal awareness of its challenges and opportunities. Finch's enthusiasm gives the WB unabridged team a great opportunity to connect design to politics, and the mayor asks his economic development director, David Kooris, to help make that happen.

Lower Manhattan

Early in 2013, HUD Secretary Shaun Donovan met with a group of influential New Yorkers and presented his plans to use Sandy to reinvent government as more responsive, nimbler, more innovative. He had barely finished speaking when he was given to understand that his vision simply wouldn't work. His audience may have liked him, but they distrusted the federal government he represented, which they saw as broken and dysfunctional. In their eyes, it would never change.

Lucky for us, not everyone felt that way. We find a powerful ally in Dan Zarrilli, who runs the Mayor's Office of Recovery and Resiliency, created by Michael Bloomberg in Sandy's wake. Bloomberg's Special Initiative on Rebuilding and Resiliency is taken over by newly-elected Mayor Bill de Blasio and comprises several hundred projects over which Zarrilli and his team have jurisdiction. He is confronted with his team's highly ambitious plan to protect Manhattan, which raises all kinds of complicated questions and requires the expertise of just about every agency in the city. Our interests overlap; he needs the same sort of comprehensive, inclusive design thinking that Rebuild by Design does. Zarilli begins organizing interagency workshops, and I smile when I hear people arriving at them ask each other, "Any idea what we're doing here?" Rebuild by Design becomes the platform for discussing Manhattan's resilience. This is valuable for everyone.

"You can't kick us to the curb when you're dealing with
something that we believe we own. If in the next phase
the design was going to be completely different, and if all
of a sudden it went from a berm to these ugly floodwalls,
we would fight this project to make it stop, and say: 'take
your money back.' We play this role until it's done and it's
done the way that's in the interest of the community."

Damaris Reyes
Interview p.232

The BIG team's vision for protecting lower Manhattan is as simple
as it is comprehensive: a sequence of adaptive flood-protection
measures running around Manhattan from West 57th Street
down to the Battery and up to East 42nd Street. It will come
to be known as "The Big U." A major consideration is how to
create protection that also serves as social, environmental and
economic assets, neighborhood by neighborhood. In the east,
big housing projects such as Stuyvesant Town dominate, and
there are multiple hospitals present. In Battery Park and on the
west side, there are more commercial interests and wealthier
neighborhoods. Each has its own needs and demands.

We find particularly active community partners in the
Lower East Side. LES Ready! is a coalition of more than twen-
ty-five community groups working not only on long-term
recovery but also focusing on preparedness, planning and
training. A low-lying neighborhood, the Lower East Side was
hit especially hard by Sandy, widely flooded and left without
power for days. Many residents ended up stranded in their apartments. The next storm could be just as devastating, or worse.

Community members
take part in the design
process for the Lower
East Side waterfront.

Among those willing to give Shaun, me, the BIG team and the Rebuild by Design process the benefit of the doubt was Damaris Reyes, executive director of Good Old Lower East Side (GOLES). If influential New Yorkers couldn't see the opportunities in what we were describing, she could, but she was wary. GOLES had been a strong community voice for years, fighting for the rights of predominantly poor residents to defend the neighborhood and ward off gentrification. She saw possibility in Rebuild by Design, but also threat—what if rebuilding for resiliency became a Trojan horse for gentrifying forces? Yes, the community needed protection from storms, but Reyes feared losing the very thing she was fighting for if she embraced our approach. We met with her again and again, building trust. Eventually she signed on to help, but her support was conditional. "We'll join you in thinking this through and working together because we see how important it is, and we do see an opportunity for our community," she said. "But you, in turn, must show us you're taking the interests of the residents here seriously. You must deliver on this promise of trust we are building."

With her commitment, she tied her political fate to the success of our work, as others had done in Hunts Point and Hoboken and elsewhere. Their commitment allied them with the federal government, which was not necessarily a popular thing to do. If the government were to fail—if Rebuild by Design were to fall short of its promises—they would be dragged down with that failure. "They would join us, but we

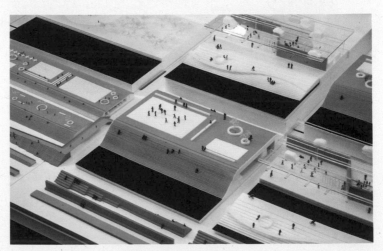

Models for different scenarios for flood protection to guide the conversation with the community, by the BIG team

knew they could easily flip sides again. She was protecting herself, which was understandable. She was also giving us a dose of reality: don't try to shake us off in the next stages, or we can become your biggest foes.

Hoboken, New Jersey

On Saturday morning, January 18, my phone rang. "What are you playing at?" demanded Marc Ferzan, New Jersey's Sandy czar and a political appointee of Governor Chris Christie. I knew what he was angry about, because I had just watched Hoboken Mayor Dawn Zimmer declare, on live television, that Rebuild by Design was going to help her in a political fight with the governor over the allocation of Sandy recovery funds.

A spat between a mayor and a governor about money is not unusual. I cringed, though, to see Rebuild by Design dragged into it as a defensive bulwark for Zimmer. This was the last thing any of us needed. Rebuild by Design had to function within a very political world, but if it became politicized it would fail utterly. Rebuild by Design did not belong to the federal government any more than it belonged to the foundations that are financing it or the grantees who were to benefit from its work, or for that matter, to Mayor Zimmer. I set up Rebuild by Design specifically as a coalition of all those different organizations. It existed on the edge of all, in the in-between, where a collective ownership could grow. Now, watching Zimmer on MSNBC, Marc Ferzan thought we were taking sides.

With Marion and Scott's help, I talked Ferzan down—MSNBC wasn't going to derail what we were doing. I knew Zimmer was taking advantage of Rebuild by Design, and I empathized with her approach and point of view. For her, Rebuild by Design presented the opportunity not just to make a comprehensive plan but also to get funding to implement the projects resulting from the comprehensive strategy, something more than some walls around Hoboken's critical infrastructure. She knew she may well never get that opportunity again. Under federal regulations, FEMA funding is reserved for rebuilding critical infrastructure. It can be used for the repair and protection of damaged fire stations, hospitals, sewage treatment plants

"With this type of project, you're dealing with a political context and you need to be able to operate within that. You're trying to reconcile what is the ideal circumstance with the political reality."

and power stations, but not for any more. You may build back, but not better. Even if you know what to change, to improve, you cannot spend that money to safeguard against future disasters—even if you can show that by protecting the entire city for future storms, you're protecting the critical infrastructure as well. Rebuild by Design offered a different path, an opportunity to deploy federal funds differently and more effectively.

Hoboken, home to a key regional underground rail station and sewage treatment plant, clearly needs a comprehensive approach. Sandy's thirteen-foot storm surge here sent water from the Hudson River pouring through city streets, which flooded up to eight feet deep. Two-thirds of Hoboken sits within the FEMA 100-year floodplain, susceptible to both flash floods and storm surges. Hoboken is the fourth most densely populated city in the country, largely brick and concrete. Any major downpour in itself is enough to flood the city from within.

Sandy showed how closely ecological, economic and societal vulnerabilities are connected. It's clear we need a collective approach to planning projects that is based on facts and realities, rather than one that chases funding that's guarded in various politicized silos. We are trying to turn the entire system of legislation, governance and financing on its head, using facts to drive design that creates resiliency for the entire region.

Analysis of interconnected vulnerabilities of Hoboken by the OMA team

Of course, Rebuild by Design can't change this system by itself. We can create a reality that shows how things can be done differently. Our sense of how to do this grows clearer every day. The OMA team is working on Hoboken's comprehensive urban climate strategy to prevent flooding, delay rainwater runoff, store and direct excess rainwater and finally remove the water from the system again. The strategy refers to the entire city, touching on hard and soft infrastructure, on community action, homeowners' investments and policy recommendations. The plan influences potential developments in many places across the city, at a granular level, to support the strategy.

We gather all the partners at Hoboken's City Hall: the OMA team, Mayor Zimmer and her staff, representatives from the state and New Jersey Transit. After the team presents the strategy and the design—illustrating the way things are interconnected and interdependent—James Weinstein, the CEO of New Jersey Transit, speaks up. "Okay, but if it is all related, what is to stop us from integrating our projects and funding? This is a great opportunity to create added value for all." OMA's comprehensive approach helps him deliver on his goals too, and can even help improve them. The logic of the narrative and the plan lead him from a fresh understanding of how things really work to the conclusion that we need to build more than individual projects scattered across the region. He can't change all the silos and the budgets, but the evolution of his understanding is a critical step for Rebuild by Design. Here is evidence that our comprehensive approach is embedding itself into the minds of our partners. We are changing the culture of the system, step by step, by design.

Costs and Benefits

As the ten teams pull their plans together, each works on four deliverables: regional research, a project, a coalition that can realize the project and a cost-benefit analysis. The analysis gives us a standard by which to compare projects to each other and will help determine how much funding to award. Yet there is no single, federal standard for doing such an analysis. Different agencies use different methodologies and often have no capability to effectively put a price on "soft" costs and benefits that matter enormously here: societal, ecological, environmental.

The need for a single, workable, cost-and-benefit approach leads us to ask members of the Interboro team, the Dutch finance and water research consultancies Rebel and Deltares, to develop a methodology for Rebuild by Design. They produce a simplified assessment that is comprehensive, forward-looking, and takes a long-term view. It incorporates the values of resilience while giving us a handle on the economic considerations inherent to each project. We know this won't give us the whole picture, but it is a tool that allows the teams, the jury that will consider the plans, and HUD itself to compare projects to each other even before we know all the details of implementation and to get a grip on their feasibility. This is another small step in what Rebuild by Design can do to change the culture, not only here but worldwide. Too often, analyses of costs and benefits don't adequately consider many of the things we are focused on. If investments in water safety also improve environmental quality and strengthen community resilience, both now and into the indefinite future, shouldn't we be able to measure and value that? It is hard to quantify the value of resilience, but if we are going to shift our stance from disaster response to climate preparedness, we should be able to factor these considerations into bottom-line calculations to show how preparedness pays off.

Comprehensive Plans, Comprehensive Presentations

In October, the teams had made "midterm" presentations to a full auditorium at the Kimmel Center at New York University—and some of them had a hard time connecting effectively with the audience. I'd watched, in the weeks leading up, how teams developed common language and understanding across disciplines and between professionals and non-professionals alike. This language bridged professional analysis and design to the benefits communities would experience from the projects. It was this collaborative and inclusive process that assured us all that we were on the right track. But when they faced a crowd of almost a thousand people, some presenters effectively froze. I could see that they were not

reaching the audience. Their presentations lacked the empathy and understanding they had developed through meetings, through debates, through being pushed outside their professional comfort zones. That day, on stage in that auditorium, we missed the chance to touch hearts and minds. Yet immediately after, off-stage in both New York and New Jersey, I witnessed much better interactions as the teams spoke in smaller and more intimate crowds—actual conversations between teams and stakeholders in which the team members were able to convey that they "got it."

We all learned from that experience. We knew that for the finals, things had to be completely different. I knew that presenting before a jury was going to feel jarring after so many months of close collaboration among and between teams, community members, and other stakeholders. We would jump from a deeply-integrated design process into a formal, juried environment. How we all managed this process was going to be critical. How could we ensure that the strength of our collective approach, so essential to Rebuild by Design and so antithetical to a typical design competition, came shining through on stage, before the jury? These presentations are formative for the jury members—the teams' chance to make a first impression as the jury begins the process of deciding who will get funding and what will be built.

To make sure that the finals are, indeed, different from the midterms, everyone practices intensely. We reconvene

Presentation of the PennDesign / OLIN team with the community of Hunts Point.

in the same auditorium, the Kimmel Center on Washington Square Park in Manhattan. Despite a brutal polar vortex that has caused the cancellation of flights and trains across the region, despite snow piled three feet high in the streets, everyone is here for two days of practice. They rehearse their performances by drawing on the power of the coalition, on the imagination and inspiration embedded in their plans, seeking not to fall back into the comfort zone of their own profession. In that empty auditorium, each team presents its project, building a narrative out of the research, the exploration, the coalition-building, the solutions they devised and why they are the best way forward, the benefits they will create.

As we get closer to jury day, we coach each team through long, intense, one-on-one rehearsals. Each must tell a compelling story, and the art of storytelling is different from the practice of collaborating with stakeholders and designing a project. They must find the narrative, the sequence, the structure and the words. Each seeks the best way to message their story, to be comprehensive and yet personal—to connect with the jury in a way that conveys both the power of the coalition and the core value of their project.

The Finals

On April 4, we gather with the jury in an extraordinary space: twenty-three floors up in a downtown Manhattan office tower, on an unfinished floor of concrete and pillars measuring fifty meters on a side, surrounded by glass. It is the world's best view, the city and the Hudson River backgrounding the presentations about places we can see if we look outside. In addition to their verbal presentations, each team has set up a comprehensive visual presentation. For two days, the jury members will read them, listen to the teams, walk the room, and read them again.

Our investment in practice has paid off. Every team has its own narrative, a compelling presentation, and a transformative proposal.

When the PennDesign / OLIN team presents, they let the community of Hunts Point do the speaking about an array of flood protection interventions they call The Hunts Point Lifelines. More than sixty people fill the stage, representing the Community Development Corporation, the food market companies and other stakeholders. They, not the designers, tell the story, giving the Hunts Point coalition a real voice in the presentation. That makes a difference; when a fishmonger raps the table and says, "Mr. Secretary, you better listen: this is good," we all sense that this is a team grounded in the community and its culture, its strategy anchored there.

Integrated flood protection, one of four Hunts Point Lifelines, by the PennDesign / OLIN team

The SCAPE team's presentation conveys how deeply their project is embedded in their hearts and minds. Their vision for protecting Staten Island makes the gigantic issues of climate change, sea

ECONCRETE
UNIT

PORE
SPACE FOR
FISH

HIGH TIDE

LOW TIDE

REEF
STREET

EXISTING SEA FLOOR
Breakwater placement avoids hard
clam habitat and other critical
species.

SUBTIDAL REEF STREET
Subtidal rock enhancements
provides structure for juvenile
finfish and lobsters.

INTERTIDAL REEF STREET
Intertidal shallow water rock enhancements for juvenile fish, lobsters, and mussels.

UPLAND ISLAND
Exposed island habitat free from predators can be used by seals and birds.

CONSTRUCTED TIDE POOL

HARD CLAM

SUBTIDAL ROCKY SUBSTRATE
Subtidal shallow water rock enhancements for juvenile finfish, lobsters, and shellfish.

MUDFLATS
Zones of moderate sedimentation create habitat for hard clams, benthic fish, and eelgrass.

level rise and ecological vulnerability small and manageable—a powerful achievement. The links between the ecology of the bay, design and engineering of their breakwaters, the resilience of the coastal community and the education program, are just right. They question the relationship between man and nature, between culture and ecology. Living Breakwaters is a representation of building with nature in its best sense: a new reef, man-made but supporting nature; a new bay for increased ecological quality, safety and community resilience; and all of it supported by educational hubs along the beach.

The MIT CAU + ZUS + URBANISTEN team present a fantastic short movie that gives a concise view of the Meadowlands: what was there, what happened when Sandy hit, and what the future will look like. They stretch their audience's imaginative powers with their analysis and interpretation of the area, but even more so through their design for New Meadowlands. Their vision is large-scale, stretching across the whole Meadowlands with a long-term strategy to ensure safety for all. Because the whole project can never be financed with their share of the "up to a billion" dollars Shaun Donovan has available to award, they must propose the best places to start. The jury asks the team to identify one or two interventions to begin in order to tip the balance toward getting funding.

The New Meadowlands
by the MIT CAU + ZUS
+ URBANISTEN team

The Resilient Bridgeport proposal by the WB unabridged team integrates three systems: natural and fortified "hard lines" that link communities and form stronger edges in places most at risk during storms; "soft lines" of green infrastructure interventions, both on land and offshore, that reduce risks, increase development value and improve the local ecology; and "economic lines" that encompass neighborhood revitalization and economic development. Combined, the Resilient Bridgeport proposal provides a framework for resilient development of the city. No less than ten projects and five studies center around four investment zones, downtown as well as upstream. Together, the project offers an array of opportunities to address the multiple challenges of Bridgeport.

The WXY / West 8 team brings to the finals the broadest-reaching vision. Their strategy and approach is massive on all levels, impressive yet much more conceptual than any of the others. They do not show the jury an implementable project. Instead they paint a picture of a vision: Blue Dunes, a rim of new, protective barrier islands, stretching beyond the New Jersey and Long Island coastline. It is designed to reduce storm surge impacts on the mainland, increase ecological quality and even bring economic opportunities. This approach is reminiscent of the massive New Deal era public works of the 1930s. Blue Dunes would require years of more research, decades to implement. It is not so much a city or state project as a federal one. The team is ready to take big next steps, yet implementation would definitely require much more research and in-depth design. That is what they ask: fund our follow-up research. I am surprised when they don't sway the jurors. What a message this project would send to the world: a physical manifestation of Dutch-American leadership at the front of climate adaptation! With a president in the White House who believes deeply in science and who wants moonshot approaches, the opportunity seems self-evident. For the jurors facing hard decisions, it isn't. But I suspect the story of Blue Dunes is not over yet.

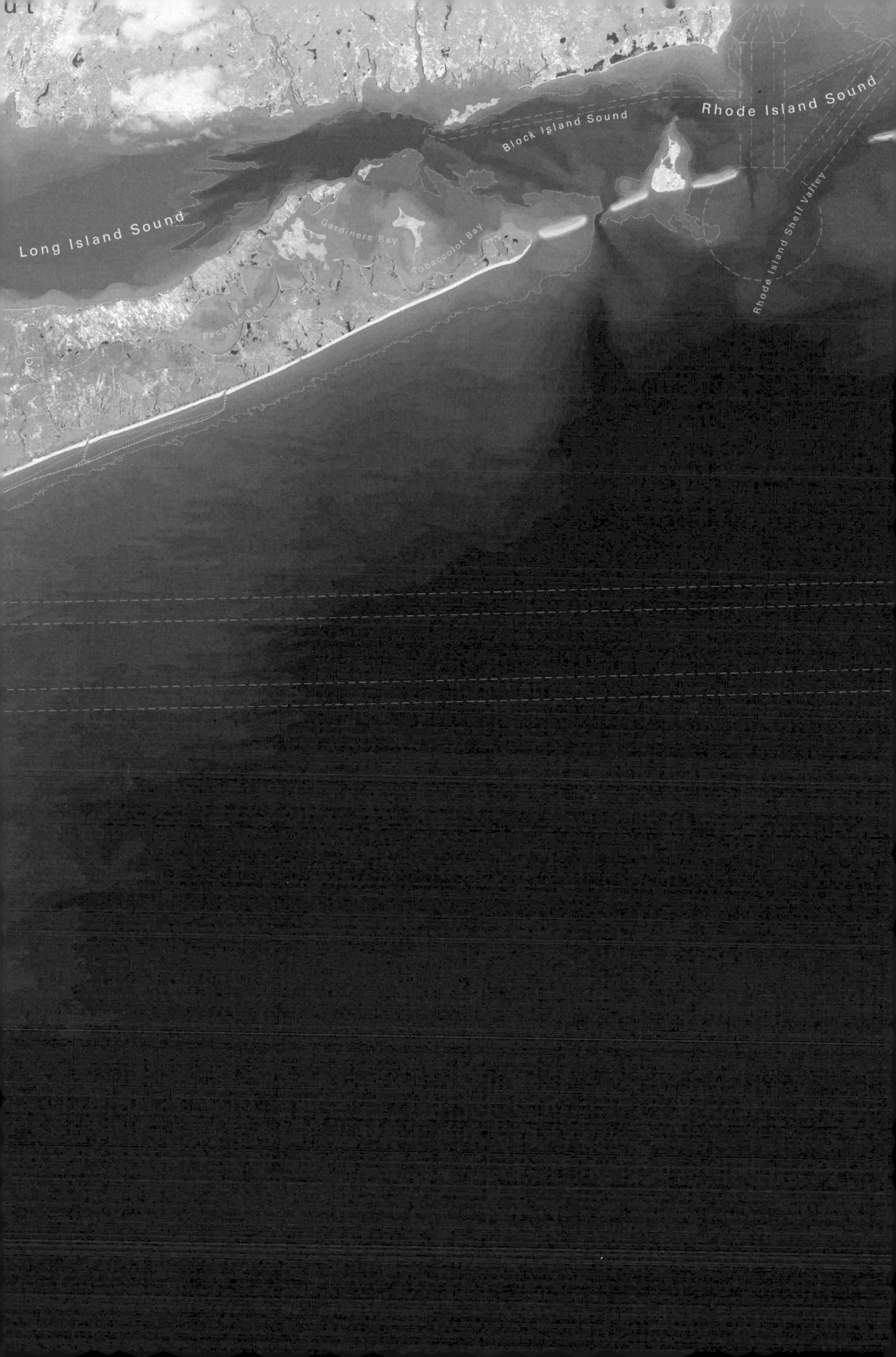

Long Island Sound

Gardiners Bay

Peconic Bay

Tobaccolot Bay

Block Island Sound

Rhode Island Sound

Rhode Island Shelf Valley

Interboro and their collaborators stay true to their analysis. Political divisions notwithstanding, Long Island is a single system: if we want to understand what's going on, we have to look at the coast as a whole. The rivers, bay and barrier islands, the currents and tides, together have an internal logic. If we understand that system and respect rather than fight it, if we build with nature and intervene intelligently, then we can live with the water. We can develop even in such a vulnerable place as the south shore of Long Island. They call their solution Living with the Bay and propose interventions at a number of locals. They do not, however, favor any of them. Instead, they present a catalog of solutions: inland, bayside and oceanside. All are needed, but not all will be built right away. Interboro's strategy in presenting this way to the jury is a risky one, for it lacks a big, important keystone project. They aren't willing to compromise on their systems approach, and that's powerful and seductive in its own way.

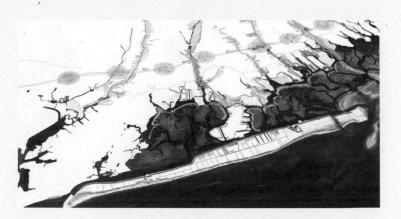

Living with the Bay: the Interboro team's systems approach of ocean shore, barrier island, saltwater marsh, river estuary, and highlands

The team of HR&A with Cooper, Robertson & Partners carried their strategy to the end, matching financial complexity with building guidelines and scaling up with urban interventions for the three sites encompassed by their project: Red Hook, Rockaway and Asbury Park. They aimed to understand what was at risk in the threat to small businesses and worked to capture that financial risk in an investment opportunity informed by urban design. The team's ask for funding from CDBG-DR addresses four levels: the tenant, the building, the corridor and the district. Their proposal for a small business resilience fund and a technical assistance program to support businesses in accessing other capital, distinguishes itself by its programmatic character, focused at the individual business and leveraging other resources. Accompanied by developments at the district and corridor scale and urban investments like the reconstruction of Liberty Warehouse and the flood protection in Red Hook, the strategy aims for comprehensive community revitalization.

The OMA team's strategy for Hoboken harmonizes design, engineering and politics. Consequently, the designer, the engineer and the mayor tell this story together. The proposal is not so much a design as it is the city's resilience strategy, stitched to its neighbors Weehawken to the north and Jersey City to the south along the western shore of the Hudson River. The components of the strategy—Resist, Delay, Store, Discharge—highlight Hoboken's climate challenges: keep the water out, slow storm water runoff, temporarily store excess water and, finally, remove the water from the system. The urban opportunities that surface when these challenges are merged in a concise and comprehensive way reveal themselves immediately. The project encompasses a catalog of interventions and a communications strategy, policy framework and process for implementation.

Comprehensive strategy for Hoboken: Resist, Delay, Store, Discharge, by the OMA team

The team of Sasaki, Rutgers and Arup finds its place and coalitions in Asbury Park, Raritan Bay and Barnegat Bay. Three New Jersey coastal typologies—headlands, inland bay and barrier islands—come together in one approach. Each place demands its own design strategy, each presents opportunities and challenges, yet they share a similar approach to analysis, coalition-building and moving forward. Three typologies, three places, three types of risks that if effectively addressed can serve as pilot projects for communities up and down the Eastern Seaboard. The barrier islands are vulnerable: under three feet of sea level rise, they are projected to lose half their area; under six feet, they would completely disappear. Leaving the islands entirely is tantamount to giving up, so how do we adjust to live with what is coming? For example, Asbury Park celebrates beach culture with an iconic boardwalk—can a more organic rendition increase environmental robustness? Can this new coastal defense become an attraction, a catalyst for economic growth? The team proposes a voluntary retreat approach by creating awareness and increasing opportunities on higher grounds, such as in the headlands.

It's great to see the BIG team's culture of young leadership resonating with their presentation. Although Bjarke Ingels, in many ways the rock star of the architectural world, kicks off, it's Jeremy Siegel, the young project leader, who takes the floor to present the project. If anyone knows the ins and outs of the project and the coalition, it's him. He frames the Big U

The Big U: ten miles of flood protection around Manhattan, by the BIG team

as the "love-child of Robert Moses and Jane Jacobs." The BIG team's idea for ten miles of flood protection around Manhattan requires a top-down approach but must be grounded in the fabric of the city and developed by the local communities fronting the waterline to serve their unique needs. The Lower East Side community representatives, who made clear from the beginning that their support was going to be conditioned upon being truly heard and included, make this point as part of the presentation, telling the jury, as they had told the team earlier: "This collaboration made us sit at the same side of the table. But be careful: we can easily switch to the other side again." Their dedication to the project is clear but measured; safeguarding the interests of their community comes first. And the BIG team makes this commitment the critical core of their project.

MATTHIJS BOUW, BJARKE INGELS, JEREMY SIEGEL–"This idea of combining Jane Jacobs and Robert Moses, making sure that whenever you do what's necessary, also becomes beneficial for the community, and to back it up with a process that is rooted both in the technical utilitarian aspects and in the social and mental aspects, it almost feels like it's not even an innovation. But to actually have that approach to this kind of public project turned out to be completely radical."

Matthijs Bouw

Bjarke Ingels

Jeremy Siegel

Leads of the BIG Team: founding partner of One Architecture, founding partner of Bjarke Ingels Group, project leader—designer at Bjarke Ingels Group.

JELTE BOEIJENGA What was Rebuild by Design for you?

BJARKE INGELS What was interesting to me is that in the beginning Rebuild by Design looked a little bit like something the design industry does quite often: sometimes, when there's some big issue or a crisis, funds are raised for research and some workshops that result in exhibitions, debates and conferences–rarely does this materialize into actual projects or change. I was a little bit suspicious that this could be the case with Rebuild by Design. Rather than having the freedom of everything being theory and then making some interesting visions, unrooted in any kind of reality or implementation, we are much more interested in taking something that is dead-pan utilitarian and try to make it a little more visionary. So our approach on Rebuild by Design was, that we sat down, read the Special Initiative for Rebuilding and Resiliency report, read all the recommendations and then asked ourselves: what will happen, no matter what? And can we find ways to make that happen in a way that's actually going to generate positive urban development, to make it in such a way that it's urbanistically, socially and environmentally transformative. So that it's not just pure engineering but that it's actually something different and much more. So Rebuild by Design in a way started almost in pure theory and idealism, and once the project boiled down to

what matched the *Big U*, we felt we had really gotten instrumental and almost non-innovative. This idea of combining Jane Jacobs and Robert Moses, making sure that whenever you do what's necessary, it also becomes beneficial for the community, and to back it up with a process that is rooted both in the technical utilitarian aspects and in the social and mental aspects, it almost feels like it's not even an innovation. It's common sense. But to actually have that approach to this kind of public project turned out to be completely radical. Once we got into the implementation, we realized it was actually a moonshot level of ambition.

> **"Once the project boiled down to what matched the *Big U*, we felt we had really gotten instrumental and almost non-innovative."**

MATTHIJS BOUW We tried to design our project in such a way that it could withstand that process. And it is this link between understanding the process and making the project that was very much at the forefront of what we had been thinking about for a long time. The project requires you–as a designer–to understand what it means to work in this geography. You operate in an environment that is atomized and where design can be a vehicle to overcome this atomization. You design the spatial and social environment that can create resilience. And you do that in various ways at the same time. You play a role in analyzing, understanding and communicating the vulnerabilities, you can inspire and narrate the bigger story, you play a role in integrating agendas and when necessary innovating so that this integration can be met. Through this, you can create the link between project and process, because you understand where the contested spaces are. And through that understanding you can organize the playing fields, facilitate co-creation and collaboration in many different ways and come up with different solutions. And at the end, when there's clarity, you can translate it into a principal project. So we analyzed the environment and designed accordingly. I think the crucial element was that we managed to chop up our project. We analyzed the institutional environment and chopped the project in pieces, just big enough so that the system could digest them. Knowing the way the grant was structured, how Congress had allocated the funding, and that there was a particular timeline, we designed a project that would have impact before that time. We proposed the first phase of the project where it was easiest and argued if that gets funded, it will become unstoppable and more will follow. So while we had all kinds of long-term and highly integrated visions, we realized that if we start to include them at this moment, we're not going to

have a project. So while we did not hide them in the proposal, we never put them front and center, because the environment we were working in wouldn't have been able to manage it. Much of our time, much of our work, has been spent focusing on the issue of what the City can manage. We had a lot of discussions about that, in which I learned a lot from our team. That's also why it was important that we had mostly New Yorkers on the team, so we were basically a local group.

JB   To what extent was this approach–with this intense collaboration with the community–new to the team? What was the impact of this approach on the way you ran the project?

> "We analyzed the institutional environment and chopped the project in pieces, just big enough so that the system could digest them."

BI   Obviously it has been a crash course for our entire organization in understanding public governance and especially city governance. Secondly, I think we found out that the way we worked already, that we prototype a lot, became incredibly useful in these workshops with the community. Instead of showing up and presenting a plan, we come and there's like this smorgasbord of options. That in a way creates an instant understanding that we're not trying to impose our own plan but that we are actually interested in hearing: what do you think if do this, what about when we do that? This is what we took with us the last time, and these are the new things we'd like to discuss. There was time and the resources to have a sort of incremental development with the communities.

JEREMY SIEGEL   We decided to do the same thing we do all the time in the office, as an iterative design process. Where you start with understanding what the constraints are. Understanding what the possible tools are and then iterating on them. Thinking about everything, from a basic engineering floodwall to if you take that floodwall and make it accommodate furniture, or if you integrate it into existing infrastructure, or if you make it into a building, or if you remove the FDR and make it a berm, or if you just forget about coastal protections and do buildings piece by piece, raising them. And we made models of all of those options. And we don't just do models of the idea we like the best, we do models of everything and then we put them on the table and then we discuss. So that's what we did with the community groups, and it worked very well.

"We were almost treating the community as the client, if not literally."

MB   We always came from a very soft place, and worked our way from there. For a long time we didn't bring a design to the table but brought typologies instead. If we would have brought design ideas that had a geography or a place, it wouldn't have worked. The community groups would've had the feeling of having become an object of our study, and we needed them as partners. And this was far from self-evident. The first meetings with Damaris Reyes were dramatic: "You're designers, we don't trust you, we are afraid that transformations you suggest, in the end will lead to displacement." What saved us is that we had very limited experience in water management projects and landscape architecture. If we had thought that we knew how to do these things, we would've been less curious about how other people would do it and what their agendas were.

JB   All this time you were talking to the community, but much less to the City of New York, which in the end would receive the federal dollars to develop the project.

BI   I think the novelty of Rebuild by Design was that we were almost treating the community as the client, if not literally. We started essentially with HUD and we then found additional clients during the process, like Good Old Lower East Side and many other community groups along the waterfront. So everybody we had worked with as our clients had a sense of ownership over the design. When the design was presented to the City of New York, they were paradoxically the only ones we had not worked with as our client. So therefore, there was an adoption period. So I wonder– maybe these larger projects that have such massive community impact require a different strategy. Often you see that a lot of effort and resources are spent with the decision makers and then when it's time to get it adopted by the community, the design is not accepted by the people who will actually be using it and living in the area. Whereas if you add the smallest amount of resources, and spend an extra six or nine months, you actually end up with something that is much more likely to walk through the process because it's already fully owned by the community.

> **"Imagine if we treated all highway projects or power plants with the same approach? Because eventually they will be ingrained into the communities."**

JS   That's the interesting thing, and this was super-unique about Rebuild by Design, is that it linked design firms directly with community groups as a first step. And I think that that allowed for a quite open... we didn't know what the triggers were, and we didn't have all the baggage in our heads about what to say and what not to say. And this created this very open way of engaging. So the roots that were planted during Rebuild by Design allowed this openness to persist.

BI   All of these larger projects have an undeniable human scale presence. But somehow, perhaps because of the magnitude of them, they often end up being just big grey zones on the map and that's why they land so insensitively in the local communities. And here it made sense to do it differently, maybe because the waterfront is almost a public amenity, but imagine if we treated all highway projects or power plants with the same approach? Because eventually they will be ingrained into the communities. In Copenhagen we're working on a power plant with a ski slope. There, in a way to celebrate that the power plant is so clean, we thought let's make it a public park. And because it's vertical, let's make it a ski slope. That's one thing we don't have in Denmark. And there we created this weird thing that was adopted by the power plant because they saw it as a way to express the one true benefit of their technology, that it's clean. So that's why they see an interest in it. But then, in order to make it into a park and actual ski center they are now actually setting up a foundation, with millions of euros in funds, to complete and build and operate the ski center. In that sense we almost created a second client that is now a real client, which is the foundation. Maybe historically it made sense to put a power plant somewhere else without any kind of interface with the public domain. But I think especially now that cleantech is coming back, it will be very possible to integrate these into the grain of the city and therefore the way they interface with the city once again becomes of public relevance. This can potentially change how infrastructure is used. Instead of just tolerating the negative impact of a highway overpass or a berm on the side of a highway, all these things that highways do, when actually they are just as relevant in terms of public impact as a park. Many infrastructure projects could be made much more sensitive and sensible by having this layer on them. If you were to simply stop looking at them as purely utilitarian projects and see them instead as very important and very large urban projects. So for a small extra investment you can actually turn them into almost a driver of positive urban transformation rather than the opposite.

"The climate crisis enables certain things that wouldn't be possible otherwise."

JB   What is the difference between doing this in the U.S. compared to doing this in Europe?

MB   This culture has its downside in that there's little instinct for collaboration or integration. But it has as its upside an incredible energy to get things done. That's also why we wanted to be part

of this. We were curious about the topic, the scale of things–it's a culture that I was somewhat familiar with and I knew that I could perform in. It was curiosity, I think, more than anything else. So the fact that there's no instinct for collaboration becomes an intellectual or moral or ethical driver. It started with Bjarke and I hanging out in a bar in Amsterdam talking about the complete lack of a sense of collectivity and a conversation about the agency of design in helping shape collectives and collective issues and collective solutions. So that's a real trigger, intellectually.

BI   I think in the U.S context, the local grassroots, the communities' politics are quite strongly organized but I think also somehow more polarized. They're almost ready for disagreement from the get go. Good Old Lower East Side or Lower East Side Ready were ready to defend their neighborhood from day one. You also find this distrust in Europe but more on an individual level. It requires a change of attitude, where you somehow learn to earn your trust as a designer. The good thing is that the system is very much in place here in the U.S. There is always the organization to follow up on things. Maybe more so than my experience has been in Denmark, for instance. And this polarization on a grassroots level actually also exists on governance level. Different autonomous entities butting up against each other, all these different departments, different authorities that operate in a more complex way. In Copenhagen they essentially all work for the mayor.

JB   The *Big U* is now going into implementation. What will be the biggest challenge?

"The level of integration that we are working at, is already a phenomenal task that is really stretching the city."

JS   This was also about a crisis. I do think that a lot of what we have been able to do has been facilitated by the fact that there is a common goal. If you were just to try and do an intensive six-mile long open space public improvements project on the Lower East Side, it would never ever get done. Never. Particularly with these kinds of neighborhoods, where you have a lot of super-divergent interests. But once you have this sort of existential threat, and everyone comes around to agree that you need to do something about it, you have already taken the first step: we need to protect these neighborhoods. And then the next step is if you do that, you need to do it in such a way that it becomes a good thing for the waterfront, not a bad thing. And somehow everyone can agree on that, and then everybody works on that problem. It just kickstarts it. So in that sense the climate crisis enables certain things that wouldn't be possible otherwise. And in the end, these things– better access to open space, better routes for passive mobility, better ecological value–all help to address this same crisis.

MB   The project is successful yet I think there are many things at which our project, at this moment, is not ideal, especially in terms of the long-term adaptation strategies and getting an optimal integration with all kinds of related measures. We'd like to bring the New York City Housing Authority on board in a different way for instance. And I learned to accept that not everything works out the way you intend. The possibility of these failures was built into the plan; we made the plan so that these elements can be added to the project. We should really understand and appreciate that actually doing this, at the level of integration that we *are* working at, is already a phenomenal task that is really stretching the city.

And the fact that we are succeeding in making this a positive urban transformation, rather than solely a coastal resilience project per se, is part of its success. You might say that we hit exactly the right spot of institutional capacity to make the project happen. We stretched it a little bit and we're continuing to stretch it, so we're at the right place. But a lot can be said that if we don't continue to stretch this, and address these bigger issues, then we're also failing. So one of the challenges in the coming years is, let's say, to continue to strive for a higher level of integration, continue to think through the different time scales and the different geographic scales, to keep these issues on the agenda.

▲

MATTHIJS BOUW–"You might say that wc hit exactly the right spot of institutional capacity to make the project happen. We stretched it a little bit and we're continuing to stretch it, so we're at the right place. But a lot can be said that if we don't continue to stretch this, and address these bigger issues, then we're also failing. One of the challenges in the coming years is to continue to strive for a higher level of integration, continue to think through the different time scales and the different geographic scales, to keep these issues on the agenda."

CARRIE GRASSI–"The Rebuild by Design projects were clear priorities of the city from the outset. And yes, we thought these projects needed to be inclusive, we needed to have a community process, but the design teams, they lived that. So the competition set a very high bar that was important for the city to continue. The trust that the teams built with the community was tremendous and that goes a long way in building a successful project."

Carrie Grassi

Senior Policy Advisor at NYC Mayor's Office of Long-Term Planning and Sustainability from 2012 to 2014 and since then Senior Policy Advisor and later Deputy Director for Planning at NYC Mayor's Office of Recovery and Resiliency

JELTE BOEIJENGA What was the start of Rebuild by Design for you?

CARRIE GRASSI I started in what at that time was the Mayor's Office of Long-Term Planning and Sustainability, about a month and a half before Hurricane Sandy hit. My job was to update the city's flood maps in coordination with FEMA. I remember, when I started the job, very few people outside the small team at my office cared about flood risk. And then came Sandy, which just turned everything on its head: understanding, being aware of, and needing to do something about flood risk became the primary focus of our office and the administration. Mayor Bloomberg put together the Special Initiative on Rebuilding and Resiliency and we spent six months developing the city's long-term climate resilience plan, called A Stronger, More Resilient New York, with climate change and understanding flood risk at the heart. This was issued in June of 2013 and from then on, that resilience team started to work on implementing the 270 initiatives laid out in that plan. That was about the same time the Rebuild by Design competition started, so as we were organizing ourselves around this task, Rebuild by Design was kicking off. And it was not totally clear what they were doing. We had just gone through this planning process ourselves, had done a lot of investigation into the city's flood risk, and had worked with a group of climate scientists to understand our future risk due to sea level rise and increasing frequency of large storms, and yet the first phase of the competition was about investigating risk. That was confusing for the city; it felt duplicative and a little dissociated from the work that we had already been doing. We didn't feel really engaged as partners at that stage of the competition. There was a little bit of "What is that thing? Okay, it's a big deal, we'll go along, but we don't really understand where it's headed and if it's going to be beneficial to the city in the long run." I think the moment that each design team had one project selected was when we really got engaged.

> "We were very worried that the city was going to be asked to do a project which was not funded appropriately."

JB At that moment, it also became clear that the CDBG-DR money was attached to the projects.

CG Yes, but with no idea of quantities. On one hand, this made it possible for the teams to think about holistic solutions without funding constraints. But on the other hand, some teams made a reasonable ask, but other projects were so huge that there was no way the whole proposal was ever going to get funded by the competition. And on top of that, what was a bit frustrating about the process from the city's point of view, was that we didn't really have a window into how the teams were doing their cost estimating. So we were very worried that the city was going to be asked to do a project which was not funded appropriately because the cost estimating was not done appropriately. And what we're seeing ultimately, is that the amount of funding that we received is not going to cover the entire projects. Yes, there was a desire by HUD that the grantees look for other sources of funding, but there is no other pot of resiliency funding in the hundreds of millions of dollars. So that's been a challenge, and still is.

JB   Did the competition somehow change or influence the agenda of the city?

CG   I think what was really important about the design competition, was that it wasn't just a design competition, it was a mutual process of education that both the designers and the communities embarked on together. In thinking about resiliency, it's not just: we will put this thing in place and this will protect you. Resiliency is really trying to think about future conditions and understanding the risks that we face and understanding how we can not only utilize projects for protection, but also to improve other aspects of the public realm as well, to strengthen communities. Because a strong community is one that will bounce back more quickly. So the process of the competition, I

would say, was just as important as the outcome.

> "It is something we wanted to do anyway, but we were now being held to an expectation, which is a different thing."

However, I don't think the competition changed the agenda of the city so much, because we had laid out this very comprehensive, clear resiliency plan. The East Side of Manhattan was a specified priority, the Hunts Point Food Distribution Center was a clear priority, doing erosion control was a priority project. So the Rebuild by Design projects were clear priorities of the city from the outset. But we didn't really have an engagement process at that time. We were just setting out to start the implementation. And yes, we thought these projects needed to be inclusive, we needed to have a community process, but the design teams, they lived that. So the competition set a very high bar that was important for the city to continue. It is something we wanted to do anyway, but we were now being held to an expectation, which is a different thing. I think the teams laid a lot of amazing groundwork for the city for that. The trust that they built with the community was tremendous. A lot of people in these neighborhoods were fully involved and engaged and that goes a long way in building a successful project. I'm not sure the city would have been able to spark that kind of excitement if we had been the initial touch point. And we're being watched by folks beyond the city. Because of the high-profile nature of the competition there are a lot of people who are familiar with these projects, and they want to know about the progress. It's that attention that helps keep the aspirational goal of resiliency in the mind's eye of the public.

JB You say the city had to respond. But at a certain moment the city also needed to own these projects. How did this go?

CG The teams did a tremendous amount of work in a short period of time—I don't want to sell that short at all—but they were not able to do a lot of the technical work. They handed over concepts. And we spent pretty much the first year grounding these concepts in either the technical realities of the site or reprioritizing them to fit with the allocated grant award. Our city agencies weren't engaged heavily in the competition process. They saw some ideas, gave some feedback but the real attention to the details of city assets, and what it means for the project to be built, that's been something we've had to inject into the projects. I think a lot of the city agencies felt like these projects had been foisted on them. For instance, for the East Side Coastal Resiliency project, the *Big U*, we felt we needed a lot of heavy engineering influence to ground

the project in technical realities, but we also wanted the design capacity and the vision of the competition team.

For the Hunts Point project, one of the amazing things was that the team was able to bring together groups that are not used to working with each other: the markets, the residents, the community and elected stakeholder groups. The team was able to bring everybody to the table and get folks to really work with each other. But part of why that was possible was because there was no boundary on the amount of money to spend, so everybody's priorities could have a little something. And that led to a challenge for the city when we only received $20 million for a project estimated to be over $800 million: how do we take this big thing and narrow it down and not alienate any of these groups that have come to the table? So for Hunts Point we spent the first year going through a process with the community to develop a framework for prioritization, after which the city selected two areas of focus based on that prioritization. We were a year removed from the competition when we finally had this more defined project and could put out the request for proposal for design and engineering teams.

"Being both aspirational and visionary and at the same time grounding the work a bit more in the realities of capital projects is important."

So I understand the value in having government step back to be able to build bottom-up capacity and ownership in the community, but that can create other potential problems down the road. For future competitions such as this one, I think it would be important to figure out how to include local governments earlier on and to have some boundaries on budgets and some consistency in cost estimating. Being both aspirational and visionary and at the same time grounding the work a bit more in the realities of capital projects is important.

"Resiliency is really trying to think about future conditions and understanding the risks that we face."

JB   To what extent has New York City's government, or the Mayor's Office, changed as a result of Rebuild by Design?

CG   The city's climate resiliency plan is full of initiatives that our office is working on with all of the city agencies, and a number of these projects involve some sort of coastal protection or flood risk reduction which can also be transformative for neighborhoods. What we're seeing is that there is starting to be capacity built in city agencies to work on these types of projects. Things that we've learned from the East Side Coastal Resiliency project are being brought into earlier stages of other projects, and a lot of the issues that ESCR is raising– policy questions, questions about who is responsible for this new type of infrastructure, etc.– require the city to think about its governance model, its long-term organizational structure, about how we incorporate thinking about the planning, the maintenance and operations of these projects into the structure of the city. And we have been having a lot of conversations about, for instance, the role of parks in certain projects. Are parks being used to protect the neighborhood, or are they themselves in need of protection? How do we build long-term resiliency into other public spaces? The work on ESCR has pushed these questions forward, simply because they hadn't arisen previously. We're more and more able to address them as a citywide issue rather than project-by-project, looking at it holistically: how do we think about and plan for future conditions in the city? The goal is to build this capacity into the structure of the city, and make resiliency planning for climate impacts a part of good long-term planning in general.

▲

CARRIE GRASSI–"The goal is to build this capacity into the structure of the city, and make resiliency planning for climate impacts a part of good long-term planning in general."

DAMARIS REYES–"We thought the money was ours, for our community. So we had a right to weigh in and continue to be a part of the process. And the work that we did actually helped to get the money. We organized our community, I got all my elected officials to jump on, we pushed and showed that the community really wanted this. That's why we felt ownership."

Damaris Reyes

Executive director of Good Old Lower East Side

JELTE BOEIJENGA What did Rebuild by Design mean for you and Good Old Lower East Side?

DAMARIS REYES What made Rebuild by Design unique is that we actually got the money to do it. We had been involved in a number of planning initiatives before. And every time we've issued reports with recommendations of what the community said they want, but in the end there was never any money behind it. And later you realize that these projects were not really meant to materialize into anything but were more about changing the public discourse and beginning the conversation. But this does lead to a sort of planning fatigue. So with Rebuild by Design, we got involved because we thought it was important, but I'm not sure that we fully believed that it would be funded as quickly as it has been. Also because this is the Lower East Side. This waterfront has public housing, and a lot of low-income people. So therefore, the Lower West Side gets everything. They get stuff. At least that is the analysis that people have. It was unbelievable that the Lower East Side was chosen out of all the compartments. And even more unbelievable that we won so much money. It was surreal. They called us from the Netherlands to tell us. And we started screaming and crying on the sidewalk because we couldn't believe it. We won!

JB You say, "We got the money." Apparently you felt like being the owner of the project, despite the fact that officially you didn't get any money at all.

DR That's because our neighborhood got the money. And we live here. And what we did was for the people who live here, for ourselves. I think there's two things contained there. One that we thought it was ours, for our community, so therefore we had a right to weigh in and continue to be a part of the process. And the second piece was, we feel like we were an active participant and the work that we did actually helped to get the money. So when we say we got the money, we went and got the money and we got the money here. That's how we think.

> **"This is the Lower East Side. This waterfront has public housing, and a lot of low-income people. So therefore, the Lower West Side gets everything."**

We built this coalition of groups all over the neighborhood; we organized our community to be united to support us. I went to the jury presentation and I spoke and I organized all my elected officials. I got the council members, the assembly members, the borough president, all of them to jump on and send a letter to HUD. I wrote to Secretary Donovan myself. We said, "We want you to fund this." We pushed and showed that the community was behind it supporting them, and that we really wanted this. So we were the perfect way to move this thing forward. And people knew that. I think that's why we felt ownership.

JB Did you have any specific goals when you joined Rebuild by Design? What were your interests?

DR We wanted to do a couple of things. Mitigate the potential of sea level rise, or whatever would cause flooding on the ground. Second, we wanted to make sure that people that were most impacted by the flooding, who live along the waterfront and who are largely public housing residents, had a voice. That it was not just the traditional community leaders or planners that get involved. We wanted to make sure that the integrity of the East River Park remained and that the accessibility of the people who live along the waterfront or the community at large, was increased in a real way. And we wanted to make sure that whatever came was not to become a barrier for us, from the water.

Secondly, I think, we wanted to see if there were opportunities to use this process and the plan to prevent the New York City Housing Authority (NYCHA) leasing more land to private developers to build luxury houses. This is a neighborhood that has been dealing with gentrification. Anything that you do to it, even though it's great, beautiful, and we like it, it's not for us. Fixing up the park may be beautiful as a way for creating a multipurpose space. But it also makes the land across more attractive to private developers. So we tried to put in place policy or continuity of the project that included the land next to the project area. We know for example that the berm with certain storms is not going to keep all the water out, just some of it. So we thought, on the NYCHA campuses there's all this space. We should use that as a stormwater and rainwater catchment, to create permeable surfaces that can take the water in and prevent more flooding. And if we did that, we would not so much protect the buildings that are there, but protect the land from being built on. Because from then on it would not be so-called empty land anymore but would have a purpose. And although we've accomplished a lot of things, we weren't successful in that. Not yet.

> "We wanted to make sure that people that were most impacted by the flooding, had a voice."

But we wanted to at least make sure that nothing in the meantime put that housing or that land at risk, that nothing was going to happen that would cause any level of displacement, because that's where the most vulnerable of our community live. So we also told them from the beginning that we could work with them, that we believed we deserved that protection from the flooding, but that if we saw that kind of impact, we would easily go from being partners to becoming adversaries of the project.

JB   Is that still the case?

DR   Yes, that's not going to change. And it's the scariest feeling in the world. The project has created a lot of opportunities and attention. We give people tours and show them what it could look like. But then there's what it becomes, the unintended impacts. What's going to happen in 20 years? Right now, we're like woo, there's all this money, all this work is fantastic, high five Lower East Side and you guys rock. But in 30 years people may say they set these wheels in motion that ultimately became the last nail in the coffin of their community.

JB   That's the long-term fear. I can imagine there must also be a short-term fear, or at least hesitation. You say to HUD there are no guarantees for continuous support, but you still have become part of the project. Or not?

DR   We are good at being partners and not being partners. We've been working on this for two and a half years now and we've been supportive to the extent that even now when we have meetings, I don't go in there and say this is fantastic, oh my gosh, this design is amazing. We're mostly asking questions: who's going to do the outreach? Where is the community? Where are the public housing residents? Where do they weigh in? So we still play that role and raise those issues.

We're going into the next phase now, as the process continues to evolve. And you know, things start one way and end another. The process under Rebuild by Design was one thing. Then the process under the East Side Coastal Resiliency was another. Once the competition phase was over and the money was awarded, the project went to the city. And it was like the city had short-term memory loss. They issued contracts to other groups to do the community engagement and these groups reached out to us about how to do their work. At the first meeting after the project went to the city, a bunch of us just said, "What are you doing? You already have dates for meetings and you already know what you're doing and then you ask us to bring the people? We don't think so." That was the first meeting. But I will do that. I have to be the guard for my community, I like that.

> "In 30 years people may say they set these wheels in motion that ultimately became the last nail in the coffin of their community."

JB   But apparently you were also in a position at that moment to influence the process and make the city realize they should change course.

DR   At some point we managed to get on track. And get it right. But there was a moment when we thought oh, they won, not us, the city has the money, now they're going to kick us to the curb. I think they don't understand: you can't kick us to the curb when you're dealing with something that we believe we own. So let's say that if in the next phase the design was going to be completely different, and if all of a sudden it went from a berm to these ugly floodwalls, we would go crazy. Then we would fight this project to make it stop, and say, "Take your money back." So we play that role until it's done and it's done the way that's in the interest of the community.

> **"I felt like they understood the fears that we had. And that's why I was able to go with them to the jury and say: listen, this is what my community asked for."**

But we have faith in the designers. If the BIG team hadn't been chosen for the first phase of the East Side Coastal Resiliency, I don't know if we would have moved forward with the same... it would have been like starting from scratch for us. At least BIG knew who we were and we knew who they were. Believe it or not, even though there's always project managers and all these other things, the designers

and us, in some ways we check in. Because the designers want to make sure that they're reflecting the neighborhood. The designers know we are bringing the community and that we're watching. And so we built a level of mutual... I think... trust? And I think we tried to guard that and make sure still.

JB   What made this trust grow?

DR   When people do what they say they are going to do. It's not that hard. When you say we're listening, we hear you, and then they come back. You know what they went through? To have meetings with the community, hear, change it again and be ready to come back again, wanting to get more feedback and change it again. And then when they came back, you could see reflected in the design what the community was saying. You could just see it. They wanted to know what we wanted, and they wanted to know that they would deliver what we wanted. They wanted to know we were happy. I felt like they understood the fears that we had. And that's why I was able to go with them to the jury and say: listen, this is what my community asked for.

▲

DAMARIS REYES–"If in the next phase the design was going to be completely different, and if all of a sudden it went from a berm to these ugly floodwalls, we would go crazy. Then we would fight this project to make it stop, and say, 'Take your money back.'"

PART V
Moving Forward
May—September
2014

The Judging: Design Plus Politics

We want the jury process for Rebuild by Design to be innovative in the same way other aspects of our work have been. In a typical competition, a jury's members would fly in, spend two days listening to presentations, and then judge the project against criteria we had devised. We wish to be more comprehensive and collaborative than that, so in the months leading up to jury day, we conduct several meetings with the jury to discuss the criteria for judging projects and the selection process itself. We have asked these individuals to jury the Rebuild by Design because we believe they are the top experts on resilience and design, and we want to put that expertise to work in developing our criteria. In our group conversations with jurors we ask: What is the minimum they should expect in terms of resilient design, and what do they hope the teams will actually present? How do they envision reaching their decisions? How can they push the teams to the limit on their deliverables? Rebuild by Design follows

"Understanding what the politics are potentially puts you in a place where you have a better chance of success. Rather than saying design and politics are completely separate, or design judgment is good and political judgment is bad, they're both reality and we brought them together in the conversations."

Shaun Donovan
Interview p.46

a learning curve; we can learn from the jury itself as we develop the evaluation process.

Shaun gets involved in these discussions, which are as open and transparent as we can make them. He educates the jurors in the political reality surrounding these projects so they may incorporate that understanding into their deliberations. Yes, he explains, the relationship between New Jersey, New York and New York City matters and is politically relevant to the distribution of Community Development Block Grant Disaster Recovery funds. And yes, if a project has strong popular support it's more attractive to the state or city responsible for implementing it.

Shaun wants to chair the jury himself, which raises juridical questions inside HUD. The agency's lawyers are concerned about any potential appearance of Shaun illegally influencing decisions on block grant spending by states and cities, something the law says he can't do. As HUD Secretary and chair of the Sandy Task Force he should, according to the lawyers, keep an official distance from the jury process. The opportunity for fraud in the awarding of funds for real estate and land development is real, so Congressional oversight committees will pay close attention to what we do. Shaun has to avoid any appearance of impropriety. In the end, after just about every lawyer in HUD examines the situation, they agree that jury members can advise Shaun individually but not collectively. With the benefit of their expertise and insight, he alone will make the final decisions about which projects are funded. It is a small win against the system.

In theory, Shaun could fund ten winning projects—or none. We told the teams from day one that they are not competing against each other, they are competing against a common standard of excellence, value and feasibility. They are competing to be ground-breaking and transformative. That's what Shaun desires to fund. We are seeking implementable proposals that set a new standard for resilience within our communities, proposals that inspire through design excellence and transformative change, that we can replicate and scale up across the region, the nation, even the world. We seek a set of winners that build a narrative together, each adding their perspective and their specifics to the common ambition of Rebuild by Design.

Through the course of the team presentations on April 4 and 5, the power of the designs comes through. The teams' work really has evolved into compelling narratives—stories about the region, the people, the risks and the possible rewards. The jury is fascinated by each presentation and taken in by the visual representations of what the designers have in mind— even if they aren't always entirely convinced. Top-level political players come to our downtown space during these two days, representing the grantees, the White House, the Office of Management and Budget, Department of Housing and Urban Development, Department of Transportation, Federal Emergency Management Agency, and others. Politics under pressure is real politics, and I can see it working as the forces in the room align themselves toward decision-making. The designs now live in the minds of the people who are to get the job done. The projects are no longer abstract ideas. Some of the concepts presented in here are going to be built out there, beyond the plate glass windows.

As the formal presentation period comes to a close, we make a promise to the teams: we'll have funding decisions in a month, maybe a few days longer.

Time to Select: Distributing the Funds

Six projects emerge from our deliberations: New Meadowlands in the New Jersey Meadowlands; Resist, Delay, Store, Discharge in Weehawken, Hoboken and Jersey City; Living with the Bay in Nassau County on Long Island; Living Breakwaters on Staten Island; The Big U on Manhattan; and Hunts Point Lifelines in the South Bronx. They are transformative, inspirational, politically-valid projects that Shaun can work with. We have winners.

Now there is the matter of funding. Incredibly, even at this late stage, we don't know if we will get any money for these projects at all. If the process to date hasn't been exciting and stressful enough, it certainly is now. The cumulative price tag for these six projects is $1.9 billion. The one thing that is not in question is that we will not have $1.9 billion to spend. In fact, we may have nothing. Not a single dollar has yet passed from the federal government to Rebuild by Design. Whatever funding the projects will receive comes from the third and final tranche of Community Development Block Grant Disaster Recovery funds, which HUD will distribute in mid-2014. There are multiple demands for this money from many fronts, including the National Disaster Resilience Competition (NDRC), which has significant support inside HUD. There remains opposition to our entire approach. The biggest threat is a pile of unfunded requests from cities and states that have other Sandy recovery work to do. There simply is not enough money to pay for them all.

Everything, in other words, is still up in the air. Once again we find ourselves explaining why this is the best way to spend part of the federal recovery funds, why we need innovative projects to help build resilience, how we got to those projects collaboratively, and how they respond to HUD policy objectives and local needs. We go through it all again, seeking a renewed commitment from HUD, from Capitol Hill, from the various agencies and governments involved so that we could get to a funded decision on the winners.

Together with HUD staff, the grantees and the teams themselves, we review the probable winners, as we have taken to calling the six projects, over and over again. Donovan will choose to fund one project, or six, or anything in between. We all want him to fund all six, if at all possible. If that is to happen, we must redefine the first phases of some of the projects to make them more feasible and affordable. We look at each project and ask, can we break off a smaller piece to fund first, keeping in mind where the need is greatest and what the project brings to address that need? In talks with the grantees,

one question always comes up: is there enough support for this selection? In other words, will you still embrace it if we redefine the first stage? Implicit in that question is another one: will you see it through? The success of many of these complex projects depends on the follow-through by the grantees after Rebuild by Design wraps up and our funds are spent. Without local ownership, ongoing funding from other sources and continuous resilience work, they will fall apart. We can't fund the beginnings of projects if we aren't confident they will be carried to the end. For us to choose to fund only part of a project, it must have validity over time, both technically and politically.

Both New Meadowlands and the Big U are very large projects that take a long-term approach predicated on incremental implementation. The logical place to start the Big U is on the Lower East Side, where the community has been involved from the start and has taken ownership. This clearly is the best place, and the best community, to kick it off. New Meadowlands is more complicated, as there is no obvious place to start, no clear standout among the many communities that support the approach. The different boroughs and interests fear that if the project is not started in their locality they will not see any follow-up funding. Nevertheless, we need a pilot project and so we choose one, with the intention of scaling up.

Inadvertently, perhaps, the jury has created a politically useful situation in New Jersey. None of the proposals for the Jersey Shore made the list of probable winners, even though the shore was hit hard and Governor Christie has promised to invest in that iconic area. Because no one here appears to be a likely winner, no one faces the disappointment of losing out to a neighbor. This removes the awkward scenario of rewarding one place and disappointing others, reducing the political risk around Rebuild by Design for Christie and for HUD. There remains a credibility risk within the communities of the Jersey Shore for Rebuild by Design—after all, what have we actually done for them?—but we remain committed to finding ways to work there.

Hoboken's Resist, Delay, Store, Discharge is a clear winner, embraced not only by its enthusiastic mayor, Dawn

Zimmer, but also by Christie's office, which sees an opportunity to create a regional strategy encompassing Weehawken and Jersey City. The first phase would be built in Hoboken. Donovan is certain we'll find private funding to couple the HUD investments. This is city-making in the "sixth borough" of New York, and that means there's a good business case to make for investment. Donovan presses the New Jersey team and Mayor Zimmer: how big a risk can HUD take when awarding a prize? Do they dare take on this project without it being fully funded? Can they count on private sector involvement, and how much?

Staten Island's Living Breakwaters attracted early support from New York Governor Andrew Cuomo, and that influences the funding approach. Although the island is part of the City of New York, we propose granting funds to the state. Most of the project will take place in state waters, and the state will be the key partner during permitting and implementation. The SCAPE team has outlined a smart and doable first stage—a pilot with immediate impact and educational capacity that can be scaled up later. Their strategy combines all aspects of inclusion and comprehensiveness: risk reduction, ecology, education and local culture.

Living with the Bay is much more complicated; teasing out a pilot project is challenging. The plan is a comprehensive and thorough regional strategy for big parts of Long Island, an accretion of many different interventions at various places and scales. Collectively, even the first phases of the various projects would require far more money than we have, and the team itself didn't propose a starting point. In discussions with the jury we agree on one: Mill River, where the project will showcase the Dutch "Room for the River" approach to riverine resilience in the United States.

For Hunts Point Lifelines, we conclude—along with the City of New York—that at this stage the proposal isn't focused enough to call it a project. The challenges are amazingly well defined, the response, less so. Problems here stretch well beyond tremendous climate and flooding vulnerability to massive and divisive socioeconomic challenges. The PennDesign / OLIN project provides a great toolbox to take decisions, but it requires next steps and a different follow-up process. This is something we all want to make happen, and the city wants to co-invest to bring Hunts Point forward.

Delays, Doubts and Resolution

Six weeks have passed since we promised the presenting teams that we would have funding decisions within a month. There are whispers among the teams and their community partners that we're not going to be able to get this done, that the politics in Washington D.C. will kill it, negating all the hard work we've put in. I know that Shaun is working the political angles to nail down the funding, and we have to be patient, whatever the doubts. We have to play the game. We have a solid plan for spreading more than $900 million through the region, and the teams are anxious to get to work with community partners who feel almost like family at this point. But there's no point in forcing a decision that is not supported and owned on every level.

In the end, Shaun comes through, and HUD agrees to distribute $930 million across seven projects. Shaun rightly adds in a grant to the Resilient Bridgeport Project for a pilot project and continuing research in Connecticut. It is all good. On June 2, we make it official with announcements in New York

Little Ferry Mayor Mauro Raguseo in Little Ferry, New Jersey and HUD Secretary Shaun Donovan join New Jersey Governor Chris Christie to announce New Jersey's winning projects.

New York City Mayor Bill de Blasio, The Rockefeller Foundation Vice President Zia Khan, New York Governor Andrew Cuomo, U.S. Senator Chuck Schumer, and HUD Secretary Shaun Donovan gather on June 2, 2014. to announce the winning proposals for New York City and State.

and New Jersey, attended by Mayor Bill de Blasio, Governors Chris Christie and Andrew Cuomo, Senator Chuck Schumer, Shaun Donovan, local politicians, community leaders, The Rockefeller Foundation and our other coalition partners, and of course the teams themselves. It is a full day of emotions, dominated by a great sense of relief. Almost a year earlier, when we stood on stage with the Sandy czars from New York City, New York State and New Jersey, no one truly understood what we were starting. Today, the reality is sinking in: We are going to build resilience!

Transfer Ownership and Ambition

The last step is to write the federal notice for awarding the third tranche of the Community Development Block Grant Disaster Recovery funds. It's a remarkable process, exemplary for the federal approach and culture. In the notice, the federal government formally announces that the grantees are eligible for a grant, under certain conditions. The grantees must then draw up an Action Plan that meets these conditions and in which they describe how they intend to spend the money. The federal government can't dictate to a grantee how to do their job. It can provide guidelines, but there's little it can enforce. It's up to the grantees to present a plan; that's how the responsibilities are organized. These are the last steps in the process by which the federal government, through Rebuild by Design, has inserted itself as never before into decisions normally left to states and cities. What we have done, by creating so much collaboration up and down the chain, has challenged traditional power structures. Now, the federal notice will tell the states and cities what to spend the money on, without spelling out how to do so, guiding them in a way that respects the federal protocols for providing and spending funds yet ensuring that the Rebuild by Design projects are built as intended.

Everything depends upon the conditions in the federal notice. What do we include and what do we leave out? How do we position the designs, the design teams and their coalitions for the follow-up process? After all, the Action Plan is the basis for contracting out the follow-up stage. What can the incentives be? In short: what is the legal construct that will ensure that the ambitions and visions of the projects will actually be achieved?

OCT 16, 2014.   DEPARTMENT
OF HOUSING AND URBAN DEVELOPMENT

Third Allocation, Waivers, and Alternative Requirements for Grantees Receiving Community Development Block Grant (CDBG) Disaster Recovery Funds in Response to Hurricane Sandy

SUMMARY: This Notice advises the public of a third allocation of Community Development Block Grant disaster recovery (CDBG–DR) funds appropriated by the Disaster Relief Appropriations Act, 2013 (Pub. L. 113–2) for the purpose of assisting recovery in the most impacted and distressed areas identified in major disaster declarations due to Hurricane Sandy and other eligible events in calendar years 2011, 2012 and 2013. This allocation provides $2,504,017,000 to assist Hurricane Sandy recovery. Included in this allocation is $930,000,000 to implement projects from the HUD-sponsored Rebuild by Design competition, described in Federal Register Notices 78 FR 45551 (July 29, 2013), and 78 FR 52560 (August 23, 2013). [...]

"It's the hardest to quantify in some ways, but it could ultimately be the most powerful, that you change the people whose capacity is to then create more innovation in other realms."

Shaun Donovan
Interview p.46

Meanwhile, HUD assembles a team in New York that will work with the grantees on implementing the projects. Rebuild by Design's project manager, Amy Chester, with additional support from The Rockefeller Foundation, puts another team in place to help the design teams and communities move forward. On a related front, we continue to move the National Disaster Resilience Competition forward. Modeled along the lines of Rebuild by Design, again supported by The Rockefeller Foundation and their vision for "resilience academies," it is intended to apply to any region of the United States affected by a disaster in the years 2011, 2012 or 2013. The federal government is taking this work seriously and learning fast. This in itself sends an important message to the grantees, that they have been part of an inspiring example, part of creating the benchmark for resilience innovation and the best reference to date as the federal government sets out to build upon our collective experience. True, there has been no implementation yet. The work to be done is a promise, but it's a real one, with local, regional and federal ownership and real funding.

Rebuild by Design is no longer an experiment; it has become the first step in a broader process of driving change through the federal government. The Urban Institute completes its independent evaluation of Rebuild by Design, adding to our own insights. These evaluations matter; it's important to institutionalize lessons learned and exploit opportunities for change. The federal government has taken a step forward on climate adaptation, resilience and collaboration, and the grantees feel this. Their interactions with federal agencies have changed, even outside the task force and in other areas than the management of Hurricane Sandy aid. There is a collective desire among the grantees to work together, to be transformative and to dare to change.

For all that progress, I fear for the future of the Rebuild by Design projects. They are still nascent, and they will battle institutional headwinds. After the sundown of the Hurricane Sandy Rebuilding Task Force, the federal agencies with which we collaborated seem to have retreated into their silos, reverted to their old ways of operating. Now that we're in the implementation phase, I wonder if we shouldn't continue to work around the existing frameworks and institutions as we did during the design phase. The projects are the result of an intense experiment, incubated in a specific, dedicated environment—shouldn't they be implemented in the same exceptional way? Won't we otherwise risk losing everything we just gained? The implementation has not started yet, no deals have been made, no teams contracted by the grantees. Nothing is set in stone. Do we need, again, a detour around the institutional lock-in, or are the projects sufficiently strong enough to withstand the opposition they will face once they are subjected to existing frameworks, procedures and governance structures? Or do I underestimate them? Do they have the potential to change the system through their transformative capacity?

Kate Orff

Founder and Partner of
SCAPE

"During Rebuild by Design, the 'Photoshop-style' perspective images that were produced by all the teams were so heavily promoted that there was something of backlash. How is this different from any other competition? That was a challenge. Because who wants to say no to the vision or the image? But how is it tied into real needs and implementation pathways? You need images to inspire, and it's important to get things out in front of people, but you can hide things in renderings–you can hide the reality of funding, of construction–a rendering is sometimes falsely holistic. And then, if you actually do a measured cross-section, you see, 'Oh, that triggers twenty regulations.' There's this whole array of legal codes at both a global level and a very local level, that essentially make resilience illegal or prohibitively expensive. There's an entire suite of legal and agency code requirements that are effectively making it impossible to upgrade the urban landscape. So the key source of innovation in Rebuild by Design was that the teams generated a set of ideas that would spark these difficult discussions. That's why I'm a true believer in architecture and landscape architecture in every sense of the word—it has a plan and a section. It's only when the rubber meets the road, when you're actually on the ground doing something and have something on the table, that you have a meaningful conversation: 'Actually, this breakwater can only be four feet above the mean high-water line, well, actually it needs to be another 100 feet away from our navigation channel,'– the details become generative. The goal with all of these projects is that you have to test them, and if you're unable to get a kind of true pilot that can be referred to as a precedent, then it's really not successful. We need this whole suite of built examples to point to in order to forge implementation pathways of the future—you can build on precedent. So the outcome of Rebuild by Design is going to be the projects themselves, but moreover it's going to be the conversations, the regulatory reforms, the modeling processes and the precedents that will then set the table for other, future projects—five or fifty years from now. That is the true result and the big takeaway."

Tentatively, yes, they do. Nevertheless, I am convinced that they remain vulnerable to failure with so much yet to do, so many steps to take, and a lack of certainty on many levels.

I consider whether we need to create an implementation agency dedicated to shepherding our seven winning projects into being. In June, I read a New York Times op-ed by Ted Steinberg titled Can the Port Authority Save the Planet?, and it gets me thinking about regional governance structures, which are common in the Netherlands. Humans tend to create artificial borders for social and economic purposes, but our cities and regions are unconstrained by these. In the Netherlands, we have had regional water authorities that cut across human-made divisions since the twelfth century—they are the basis of our democracy. Steinberg, in his Times article, explained how urban and economic challenges due to climate change increasingly manifest themselves on a regional scale, citing New York, Bangladesh and Hong Kong. He argued that regional interdependencies demand regional governance and made the case to strengthen the Port Authority of New York and New Jersey's capacity to integrate and operate more holistically. Wouldn't it be great if we could reinvent the Port Authority as a regional platform to oversee and safeguard the implementation of the Rebuild by Design projects? I bring the idea up with friends in New York and New Jersey and am almost laughed out of the room. As a foreigner, I fail to understand the history and controversy surrounding the Port Authority, which various people see as corrupt, incompetent, or both. "Not in this region," my friends say. "Not with this politics, this history, this Authority."

So it will be up to us. The projects must stand on their own, bolstered by the communities and politicians that have embraced them, the funding they have attracted so far, and their ambitious vision to drive change with the grantees. I look forward to the day when they are built and we can begin replicating them across the region, spreading resilience. These seven inspirational and transformative projects, with funding to implement their first phases, enjoy immense, ambitious political commitment from federal agencies, the states and the cities across the region, their communities, and the full support of the president. We have helped develop capacity among all our partners, now organized in inclusive and strong coalitions at various scales. Now the onus is on the grantees, the cities and states receiving $930 million: Can you deliver on our mutual promise? We made a pledge together, to each other and to the region. This is our joint responsibility. Take up this challenge, draw up an ambitious Action Plan, and we will work with you again.

We who created Rebuild by Design had a vision to use a competition to change the world. We needed many factors to align: political will, talent from many arenas, a visionary president, inspired coalitions and a devastating disaster that created this opportunity. We all take pride in what we have accomplished with Rebuild by Design through inspirational design work. We are confident that we stayed true to our ambitions to help wounded communities and leapfrog an entire region into a more resilient future. We did it, and we can do it again. We will do it again.

Act Now

Act Now

We have no time to waste. Every indecisive
day means more despair, more disasters and
less time to mitigate and adapt. The situation
is worsening fast and improving it is becoming
more costly by the day. As President Obama
said, "We are the first generation to feel the effect
of climate change and the last generation who
can do something about it." Our knowledge and
understanding of that future and our capacity to
intervene and act have never been this great. We
know just about everything that can go wrong
and possess all the resources and skills to do
something about it. So the biggest disgrace is
to look the other way. There is no excuse at all. It
is our only chance for a future and our biggest
obligation. We must dare to embrace that future
in all its complexity, dare to understand it and
exploit it for real change. It can and must be done,
now. It only requires the will to act and the guts to
change. Nothing else.

Act Now

This asks for leadership and ambition that reaches beyond ourselves, all over the world, in every situation, organization and context, be it personal, institutional, public or private. With our governments taking responsibility for the societal base by mitigating extremes and creating a level playing field for collaboration. With real knowledge, experience and understanding, investing in partners and networks, with both feet firmly in the community. For business, academia, NGOs and foundations, for collectives, institutions and individuals, the challenge is no different. This calls for leadership that draws its responsibility from understanding the world's needs, out of conviction, dedication and with ambition.

Act Now

Ultimately, this calls for action, by everyone. It isn't easy, and everything is always different, but that is no excuse, ever. Eventually, every context is backed up by people, including a culture in which risk aversion, ignorance and a lack of ambition are rewarded. And it is that culture, that institutional bankruptcy we need to get rid of. And we all shoulder that responsibility.

It is not so hard; try it. Make mistakes and learn. Innovate, include and integrate. Inspire! And do it over and over again. Out of conviction, belief, ambition and the need to change now, fast and all the way. Too big? Not at all. Look past the obstructions for the opportunities. Rebuild by Design was built on this premise: there is always an opportunity for change and impact. And there's only one way to take: making the effort, leapfrogging by learning, by design and deliberation, in true collaboration. We all can do this, if we have the shared will and ambition to make the world a better place.

Rebuild by Design

Hurricane Sandy Task Force and Federal Agencies
Army Corps of Engineers
Corporation for National and Community Service
Council of Economic Advisers
Council on Environmental Quality
Department of Commerce
Department of Education
Department of Veterans Affairs
Department of Agriculture
Department of Energy
Department of Health and Human Services
Department of Homeland Security
Department of Housing and Urban Development
Department of the Interior
Department of Labor
Department of Transportation
Department of the Treasury
Economic Development Administration
Environmental Protection Agency
Federal Emergency Management Agency
Fish and Wildlife Service
National Oceanic and Atmospheric Administration
National Endowment for the Arts
Occupational Safety and Health Administration
Office of Management and Budget
Office of Science and Technology Policy
Small Business Administration
White House Office of Cabinet Affairs

Partner Organizations
Municipal Art Society
New York University's Institute for Public Knowledge
Regional Plan Association
Van Alen Institute

Philanthropy
The Rockefeller Foundation
Community Foundation of New Jersey
Dodge Foundation
Deutsche Bank Americas Foundation
Hearst Foundation
JPB Foundation
New Jersey Recovery Fund
Surdna Foundation

Grantees
Governor's Office of Storm Recovery, New York
Governor's Office of Recovery and Rebuilding, New Jersey
Office of Recovery and Resiliency, New York City Mayor's Office
Department of Housing, State of Connecticut

Advisory Groups
Research Advisory Group: Eugenie L. Birch, Vishaan Chakrabarti, Thomas G. Dallessio, Ingrid Gould Ellen, Gerald E. Frug, Mindy Fullilove, Mohammad Karamouz, Klaus Jacob, Eric Klinenberg, Harvey Molotch, William Solecki
Jury Members: Hon. Shaun Donovan, Chair, Henk Ovink, Dr. Lauren Alexander Augustine, Julie Bargmann, Ole Bouman, Ricky Burdett, Dr. Susan Cutter, Jeanne Gang, Eric Klinenberg, Guy Nordenson, Mitchell J. Silver, Mark Tercek
Special Advisors: Marilyn Jordan Taylor, Jonathan Rose, Kate Ascher

Kingdom of the Netherlands
Ministry of Infrastructure and the Environment
Ministry of Foreign Affairs
Dutch Embassy in Washington, DC
Dutch Consulate in New York

BIG Team
Team Leads: Bjarke Ingels Group (BIG), One Architecture
Landscape Architecture: Starr Whitehouse
Planning and Development: James Lima Planning + Development
Infrastructure Engineering: Level Infrastructure
Energy and Structural Engineering: Buro Happold
Coastal Resilience Engineering: ARCADIS
Ecological Services: Green Shield Ecology
Cultural Resources: AEA Consulting

HR&A Advisors with Cooper, Robertson & Partners
Team Leads: HR&A Advisors, Cooper, Robertson & Partners
Hazard Mitigation/Disaster Planning: Dewberry
Economic Development: Southwest Brooklyn Industrial Development Corporation
Public Realm Design: W Architecture and Landscape Architecture

Interboro Team
Team Lead: Interboro Partners
Infrastructure Engineering: Apex
Urban and Landscape Design: Bosch Slabbers, H+N+S, Palmbout Urban Landscapes
Infrastructure Engineering: Deltares
Economics and Finance: IMG Rebel
Education: Center for Urban Pedagogy
Governance: David Rusk
Academic Research Partners: New Jersey Institute of Technology (NJIT) Infrastructure Planning Program and TU Delft Faculty of Architecture
Communication Design: Project Projects
Community Building, Economics, Finance: RFA Investments

MIT CAU + ZUS + URBANISTEN

Team Leads: MIT Center for Advanced Urbanism (CAU), Zones Urbaines Sensibles (ZUS), DE URBANISTEN
Eco-Engineering: Deltares
Infrastructure Engineering: Volker Infradesign
Graphic and Communication Design: 75B

OMA Team

Team Lead: OMA
Interaction (Creative Consultant): AMO
Water Management (Engineer): Royal Haskoning DHV
Ecology (Landscape Architect): Balmori Associates
Economics & Policy (Economic Consultant): HR&A Advisors

PennDesign / OLIN

Team Lead: PennDesign/OLIN
Community Engagement: Barretto Bay Strategies
Environmental Engineering: eDesign Dynamics
Infrastructure Planning: Level Infrastructure
Economic Strategy: HR&A Advisors
Marine Engineering: McLaren Engineering Group
Civil and Transportation Engineering: Philip Habib & Associates
Structural Engineering: Buro Happold

Sasaki / Rutgers / Arup

Team Lead: Sasaki Associates, Inc.
Ecology, Biology, and Sociology: Rutgers University
Coastal Engineering: ARUP

SCAPE / LANDSCAPE ARCHITECTURE

Team Lead: SCAPE/ LANDSCAPE ARCHITECTURE
Engineering/Planning: Parsons Brinckerhoff
Hydrodynamic Modeling: Stevens Institute of Technology
Coastal Engineering: Ocean and Coastal Consultants
Marine Biology: SeArc Consulting
Education/Oyster Restoration: The New York Harbor School
Architecture: LOT-EK
Graphic Design: MTWTF
Advisor/Author of "Four Fish": Paul Greenberg

WB unabridged with Yale ARCADIS

Team Leads: Waggonner & Ball Architects, unabridged Architecture
Landscape, Planning and Community Engagement: Gulf Coast Community Design Studio
Ecology, Urban and Landscape Design: Yale University
Coastal Engineering and Stormwater Management: ARCADIS
Affiliates: Carl Pucci, Kathy Dorgan, Robbert DeKoning, Derek Hoeferlin, Don Watson

WXY / West 8

Team Leads: WXY Architecture + Urban Design, West 8 Urban Design & Landscape Architecture
Climate Science Leads: Dr. Alan Blumberg, Dr. Sergey Vinogradov, Dr. Thomas Herrington, Stevens Institute of Technology
Risk Modeling: Andrew Kao, AIR Worldwide
Engineering & Technical Feasibility: Daniel Hitchings, ARCADIS
Financial Modeling: Kei Hayashi, BJH Advisors
Landscape Ecology: Kate John-Alder, Rutgers University
Planning & Design: Maxine Griffith, Griffith Planning & Design
Graphic Design: Yeju Choi, NowHere Office
Real Estate Development: Jesse Keenan, Columbia University Center for Urban Real Estate
Community & Planning: William Morrish, Parsons the New School for Design

STATE AND LOCAL GOVERNMENT STAKEHOLDERS

Asbury Park Planning
Department
Bergen County
Berkeley Township
Borough of Moonachie
Bridgeport Housing Authority
Bridgeport Mayor's Office
Bronx River Alliance
City of Asbury Park
City of Bridgeport
City of Bridgeport Department of
Health and Social Services
City of Bridgeport Office of
Emergency Management and
Health Services
City of Highlands
City of Hoboken
City of Jersey City
City of Jersey City Planning
City of Keansburg
City of Kearny
City of Long Beach
City of Lyndhurst
City of Middletown
City of Milford
City of Monmouth Beach
City of North Arlington
City of Ridgefield Park
City of Rutherford
City of Sea Bright
City of Seaside Heights
City of Secaucus
City of South Hackensack
City of Stamford Capital Use
Board
City of Teterboro
Connecticut Department of
Energy and Environmental
Protection
Connecticut Department of
Emergency Management and
Homeland Security
Connecticut Department of
Economic and Community
Development
Connecticut Historic
Preservation and Museum
Division
Connecticut State Senate
Deputy Chief Engineer & Director
of Land Use
District 2 New York City Council
Empire Justice
Empire State Development

Corporation
Fairfield County
Fire Department of New York
Hoboken City Council
Hoboken Housing Authority
Hoboken Office of Emergency
Management
Hoboken Planning Board
Hudson River Park Trust
Little Ferry City Government
Long Island Index
Long Island Rail Road
Long Island Regional Economic
Development Council
Long Island Regional Planning
Commission
Metropolitan Transportation
Authority
Monmouth County
Nassau County Department of
Public Works
Nassau County Executive Office
Nassau County Legislature
National Center for Suburban
Studies
New Jersey Department of
Environmental Protection
New Jersey Department of State:
Department of Environmental
Protection, Department of
Planning Advocacy, Division of
Travel & Tourism
New Jersey Department of
Transportation
New Jersey Economic
Development Authority
New Jersey Legislature
New Jersey Meadowlands
Commission
New Jersey Planning Division
New Jersey Secretary of State
New Jersey State Senate
New Jersey Transit
New York City Department of
Transportation
New York City Council
New York City Comptroller's
Office
New York City Community
Boards
New York City Department of
City Planning
New York City Department of
Citywide Administrative Services

New York City Department of
Design and Construction
New York City Department of
Environmental Protection
New York City Department of
Parks & Recreation
New York City Department of
Small Business Services
New York City Department of
Transportation
New York City Department of
Sanitation
New York City Economic
Development Corporation
New York City Housing Authority
New York City Housing
Preservation and Development
New York City Landmarks
Preservation Commission
New York City Manhattan
Community Districts
New York City Mayor's Office of
Environmental Remediation
New York City Office of
Emergency Management
New York City Office of
Management and Budget
New York City Police Department
New York Empire State
Development Corporation
New York Rising
New York State Assembly
Districts
New York State Department of
State
New York State Department of
Environmental Conservation
New York State Department of
Environmental Protection
New York State Department of
Health
New York State Department of
Planning
New York State Homes and •
Community Renewal
New York State Office of
Parks, Recreation, and Historic
Preservation
New York State Office for the
Aging
New York State Senate
Ocean County
Port Authority of New York and
New Jersey

NON-GOVERNMENT STAKEHOLDERS

Staten Island Borough
President's Office
Staten Island Foundation, District
Attorney's Office
Staten Island Council
Staten Island Assembly
Suffolk County Department of
Economic Development and
Planning
Suffolk County Department of
Public Works
Suffolk County Fire, Rescue, and
Emergency Services
Suffolk County Police
Department
Suffolk County Office of Ecology
Town of Hempstead Department
of Conservation and Waterways
Town of Hempstead Department
of Engineering
Trust for Governors Island
Union Beach
Valley Civic Association
Village of East Rockaway
Village of Freeport
Village of Lynbrook
Village of Rockville Centre
Weehawken City Council

116th St Merchant Association
Action for Community
Development
Adelante of Suffolk County
Adelphi University
Afikim Foundation
Agriculture Program
Ain't No Stopping Radio
Alchemy Park
Allen Chapel AME
Alliance for a Just Rebuilding
Alliance For The Arts
Alliance of Resident Theatres
Alspector Architecture
Alzheimer's Association
American Littoral Society
American Planning Association
American Red Cross
Amsterdam Business
Amtrak
Anheuser-Busch Distributors,
Hunts Point Distribution Center
Appleseeds, NY
Archdiocese of New York
Architectural League of New
York
Architecture for Humanity
Artemis Landscaping
Arts Horizons
Arverne by the Sea
Asbury Can
Asbury Park Press
Asbury Park Environmental and
Shade Tree Commission
Ashe Cultural Arts Center
Asian Americans for Equality
Association for Energy
Affordability Consulting
Association for Neighborhood &
Housing Development
Association of Marine Industries
AVR Realty Company
Baldwin Civic Association
Barnegat Bay Partnership
Battery Park Conservancy
Battery Urban Farm
Beach 116th St Partnership
Beach Packaging Design
Beacons of Hope New Orleans
Belle Harbor Property Owners
Association
Bellport High School Students
for Environmental Quality
Bike Hoboken

Bloomberg LP
Bridgeport Board of Education
Bridgeport Child Advocacy
Coalition
Bridgeport Daycare
Bridgeport Emergency
Operations Center
Bridgeport Neighborhood Trust
Bridgeport Regional Business
Council
Bright Temple African Methodist
Episcopal Church
Brighton Beach Long Term
Recovery
Broad Channel Athletic Club
Broad Channel Community
Bronx Council on the Arts
Bronx Long Term Recovery
Group
Bronx on the Go
Brookfield Properties
Brookhaven Baymen's
Association
Brookhaven League of Women
Voters
Brooklyn Center for
Independence of the Disabled
Brooklyn Community Foundation
Brooklyn Heights Association
Inc.
Brooklyn Recovery Fund
Brotherhood of Teamsters Local
202
Brottworks Design Studio
Bungalow Bar & Restaurant
Business Intelligence
Associates, Inc
Cameron Engineering
Canarsie Disaster Relief
Committee
Canarsie Long Term Recovery
Group
Captain Don's Nautical
Adventures, Bay Park Fishing
Station, NY
Carnegie Endowment for
International Peace
Carroll Gardens Association
Carrollton-Hollygorve Community
Development Corporation
Catholic Charities, NY
Cazzeek Brothers
Center for Estuarine,
Environmental and Coastal

Oceans Monitoring

Center for New York City
Neighborhoods

Chartier Group

Chase Bank

Child Care Council of Long
Island

Child First/Bridgeport Hospital

Chinatown Partnership

Chinese Consolidated
Benevolent Association

Chinese-American Planning
Council

Citizen's Campaign for the
Environment

City University of New York,
Hunter and Jamaica Bay Institute

Clean Ocean Action

Clemente Solo Vélez Cultural
Center

Coalition for Asian American
Children & Families

Coastal Habitat for Humanity

Coastal Protection and
Restoration Authority of
Louisiana

Coastal Research and Education
Society of Long Island

Columbia University

Community Affairs & Resource
Center

Community Development
Corporation of Long Island

Community Emergency
Response Team

Coney Island Long Term
Recovery Group

Connecticut Coalition for
Environmental Justice/HCA

Connecticut Green Building
Council

Council on the Arts and
Humanities for Staten Island

County of Hudson Division of
Planning

Creative New Jersey

Crow Hill Community
Association

Culinary Kids Culinary Arts
Initiatives Inc.

D+G Industries Inc

Deal Lake Commission

Dean Sakamoto Architects LLC

Defender Homes

Department of Planning
Advocacy

Dermot

Destination Chelsea

Division of Travel & Tourism

Donors Collaborative

DoTank BPT

Downtown Alliance

Downtown Special Services
District

Dry Dock

East End Neighborhood
Resilience Zone

East Village Community Coalition

Ecological Engineering of Long
Island

Edison Properties

Empire Justice Center

Empire State Future

Enterprise Community Partners

Environmental Quality, Hunter

EPA Region 6 Urban Waters
Partnership

ERASE Racism

Fair Share Housing Center

Fairfield Business Council

Fairfield County Community
Foundation

Faith Based Initiative Group

Family Service League

Federal Employees Benefit
Association

Federation Employment &
Guidance Service

Federation of Protestant Welfare
Agencies

Feel the Music!

Fire Island Association

First National Bank

Fisherman's Conservation
Association

Flickinger Glassworks

Food Bank for New York City

Foresee Community

Forsgate Industrial Partners

Fort Defiance Café and Bar

Freeport Church of Wazerene

Friends of Conference House
Park

Friends of Rockaway Beach

Friends of the High Line

Gans Studio

Garden Club of Long Island

Gay Men's Health Crisis

Georgica Green Ventures

Gerritsen Beach Cares, Inc.

Sandy Recovery Program

Gerritsen Beach Long Term
Recovery Group

Goldman Sachs

Good Jobs New York

Good Old Lower East Side

Gowanus Dredgers

Grace City Church

Grand Street Settlement

Great Lakes Dock and Dredging

Great South Bay Audubon
Society

Greater Bridgeport Community
Enterprises

Greater Bridgeport Regional
Council

Greater Media Newspapers

Greater New Orleans, Inc.

Greater New York Lecet /
Laborers 66

Green Faith

Green Map

Greenberg Nature Center

Greenwich Village Society

Guyon Rescue

Habitat for Humanity

Hackensack Riverkeeper

Hammer Magazine

Hartley House

Hartz Mountain Industries

Hatch Mott MacDonald

HDR/HydroQual

Health and Welfare Council of
Long Island

Heffernan Realty

Henry Street Settlement

Hill Neighborhood House

Hispanic Federation

Hoboken Boys and Girls Club

Hoboken Catholic Academy

Hoboken Chamber of Commerce

Hoboken Commuter Community

Hoboken Cove Community
Boathouse

Hoboken Day Care

Hoboken Developers

Hoboken Dual Language Charter
School

Hoboken Green Infrastructure
Strategic Plan

Hoboken Jubilee Center

Hoboken Museum CFM

Hoboken Rail Yards Task Force
Hoboken Resident Community
Hopes
Hofstra University Suburban
Studies Program
Home/Made
Hoop Dancers of Connecticut
Hope Academy
Hopes Cap, Inc.
Housatonic Community College
Howard Hughes Corporation
Hudson Riverkeeper
Hunts Point Cooperative Market
Hunts Point Economic
Development Corporation
Ice + Iran
IKEA
Il Forno Bakery
Institute for a Resilient Economy
Institute of Indian Culture
Institute on Water Resources
Law and Policy
Integrated Ocean Observing
System
Interfaith Neighbors, Inc.
International Flavors and
Fragrances
Irish Arts Center
Islip Town Leaseholders
Association
iStar
Italian-American Museum
Iwa Construction
Jacobs Engineering Group
Jamaica Bay Ecowatchers
Jamestown Properties
Jaral Properties
Jennie Curé
Jersey City Division of City
Planning
Jersey Shore Partnership
JHM Financial Group LLC
Jonathan Rose Companies
Kayak Staten Island
Kearny Point Industrial Park
Keio University
Kevin's Restaurant
Kimmel Housing Foundation
KIPP New Orleans
Kips Bay Neighborhood Alliance
Knights of Columbus
Krzysztof Sadlej
KSK Architects, Planners,
Historians Inc.

Kuchma Corps
Land Use Ecological Services
Langosta Lounge
League of Municipalities
Leg. Dave Denenberg
LGBT Community Center
Linda Tool
LiRo Group
Living Systems Design and
Planning
Local Initiatives Support
Corporation
Local New York Laborers 66
Local Office Landscape
Architecture
Long Island Association
Long Island Contractors'
Association
Long Island Housing Partnership
Long Island Road Runners Club
Long Island Sierra Club
Long Island Sound Futures
Long Island Voluntary
Organization Active in Disaster
Long-Term Recovery Group
Long Island Volunteer Center
Louis Berger Group
Louisiana Office of Community
Development
Low Income Investment Fund
Lower East Side Girls Club
Lower East Side Ready Long-
Term Recovery Group
Lower East Side Tenement
Museum
Lower Manhattan Cultural
Council
Lutheran Counseling Center
Lutheran Social Services
Madison Marquette
Make the Road New York
Maracoos
Mary and Eliza Freeman Center
Mary Queen of Vietnam CDC
Mastic Beach Property Owners
Association
Materials Conservation Co.
Meadowlands Chamber of
Commerce
Meadowlands Commission
Melillo + Bauer Associates
Mercy Learning Center
Merrick Fire Department
Metis Association

Metropolitan Waterfront Alliance
Mid-Atlantic Association Coastal
Ocean Observing System
Mile Mesh
Mississippi River Delata
Restoration Project
Mo Gridder's BBQ
Monmouth University
Mothers on the Move
Museum of Jewish Heritage
Nathel & Nathel
National Coalition for Arts
Preparedness
National Institute for Coastal
Harbor & Infrastructure
National Marine Fisheries
Service
National Museum of the
American Indian
National Wildlife Federation
Natural Resources Protective
Association
Nautilus International
Nazareth Housing
Neighborhood Housing Services
of New York City
Neighborhood Partnership
Network
New England Interstate Water
Pollution Control Commission
New Fulton Fish Market at Hunts
Point
New Haven Home Recovery
New Jersey Audubon
New Jersey Bike/Walk Coalition
New Jersey Enterprise
Development Center
New Jersey Environmental
Federation
New Jersey Future
New Orleans Coalition on Open
Governance
New Orleans Office of Coastal
and Environmental Affairs
New Orleans Redevelopment
Authority
New School for Social Research
New York Academy of Medicine
New York Building Congress
New York Chapter of the United
States Green Building Council
New York City Environmental
Justice Alliance
New York Committee for

Occupational Safety and Health
New York Resilience System Organization
New York Rising Community Reconstruction Program
New York Sea Grant
New York Seafood Council
New York Smart Grid Consortium
New York Sportfish Fererat/ SPLASH
New York Sportfishing Federation
New York Times, The Lens
New York/New Jersey Audubon
New York/New Jersey Baykeeper
NewCorp
Newport Associates
NJ.com, TrueJersey
North Hudson Sewerage Authority
North Jersey Transportation Planning Authority
Northstar Fund and Adam Leibowitz Consulting
Nuyorican Poets Café
Oak Restaurant & Grill
Oakland Beach Buyout
Occupy Sandy
Ocean Bay Community Development Corporation
Old Seaport Association
Old Town Civic
Operation SPLASH
Orange Industries
Our Lady of Mt. Carmel 21st Century Learning Center
Our World Neighborhood Charter School
Parsons New School
Pattersquash Creek Civic Association
Peconic Baykeeper
Peconic Land Trust
Phillips, Preiss, Grygiel, LLC, Pleasant Plains, Prince's Bay, and Richmond Valley Civic Association
Poko Partners, LLC
Point Lookout Civic Association
Point Partners
Portside
Powell Communications

Pratt Center for Community Development
Pratt Institute
Presbytery of Long Island
Prince's Bay and Richmond Community Association
Proactive Transportation and Planning
Project Home Again
Project Hope
Project Hospitality
Project Rebirth
Pryceless Consulting/DoTank
Public Housing Resident Network
Public Service Enterprise Group
Quality of Life Coalition
Rare Find Nursery
RDK Landscape
Real Estate Board of New York
Rebuilding Together New York
Rebuilding Together of Long Island
Recovery Management Office
Red Cross
Renaissance Downtowns
Restore Red Hook
Richmond Senior Services
Ridgefield Park
River Terminal Developments
Rockaway Artists Alliance
Rockaway Civic
Rockaway Waterfront Alliance
Rockaway Youth Task Force
Rocking the Boat
Rutgers University
Ruth Green Team
Sandyhook Pilots
Santa Energy
Sara Roosevelt Park Coalition
Save Energy Project
Scenic Hudson
Seatuck Environmental Association
Secaucus Town Council
Second City Bikes
Sheepshead Bay Long Term Recovery Group
SheerSerendipity
Sheet Metal Workers Local 28
Sierra Club
Smitty's Filet House
Snug Harbor
Society of Vincent de Paul

Soho Alliance
Solar One
Solar Thin Films Group, Inc.
Eco Homes + Cleaning Tech Solutions
South Bay Cruising Club
South End Neighborhood Revitalization Zone
South Shore Audubon Society
South Shore Bayhouse Owners Association
South Shore Estuary Reserve
South Shore Waterfowlers Association
Southeast Louisiana Flood Protection Authority East
Southwest Brooklyn Industrial Development Corporation
St Ame Zion Church
St Bernard Parish Economic Development Commission
St Bernard Parish Public Schools
St Marks Center for Community Renewal
St Stephens
Staten Island Baymen's Association
Staten Island Civic Coallition
Staten Island Green Charter School
Staten Island Historic Society
Staten Island Legal Services
Staten Island Long Term Recovery Organization
Staten Island MakerSpace
Staten Island YABC Program
Steve's Authentic Key Lime Pies
Stony Brook University Department of Geosciences
Strategic Decisions Group
Structures of Coastal Resilience
Suffolk County Alliance of Sportsmen
Surfrider Foundation Jersey Shore Chapter
Sustainable Long Island
Sustainable Society Network
Sustainable South Bronx
T&M Associates
Table Talk
Tanner Senior Center
Task Force on Emergency Planning and Response for Special Needs Populations

Tear New York
The Blk Projek
The Bridgeport Area Youth
Ministry
The Center for Architecture
The City College of New York
The Coastal YMCA
The College of Staten Island
The Council of Churches of
Greater Bridgeport
The Design Trust
The Gift is Love
The Human Impacts Institute
The Hunts Point Terminal
Produce Cooperative
Association
The Idea Village
The Nature Conservancy
The Nature of Cities
The Point Community
Development Corporation
The Trust for Public Land
The Urban Conservancy: Stay
Local
The Urban Institute
The Workplace
Together North Jersey
Tom Fox Associates
Toms River, Berkeley Township
Tottenville Civic Association
Touro Law School
Town of Secaucus
Tribeca Partnership
Trout Unlimited
TruFund Financial Services
Two Bridges Neighborhood
Council
Ukranian-American Youth
Association
Union Beach Strong
Unitarian Universalists Disaster
Responder
United Food and Commercial
Workers
United Methodist Church
United Nations International
Strategy for Disaster Reduction
United Way of Long Island
University of Bridgeport
University of Connecticut
University of Delaware
Urban Coast Institute at
Monmouth University
Urban Conservancy

URS Corporation
Vidaris
Vision Long Island
Visiting Nurse Service of New
York
Vista Food Exchange
Walsh Properties
Warehouse owners
WaterWonks LLC
West Side Community
Western Bays Coalition
Wheelabrator Technologies
Wildcat Academy Charter School
Yale Urban Design Workshop
youarethecity; The Design Trust
Youth Ministries for Peace and
Justice
Zone A New York

Lexicon

CDBG-DR
Community Development Block
Grant for Disaster Recovery

CEQ
Council on Environmental Quality

DOT
U.S. Department of
Transportation

FEMA
Federal Emergency Management
Agency

HUD
U.S. Department of Housing and
Urban Development

IPI
Office for International and
Philanthropic Innovation

IPK
Institute of Public Knowledge at
New York University

MAS
Municipal Arts Society

NEA
National Endowment for the Arts

NOAA
National Oceanic and
Atmospheric Administration

OMB
White House Office of
Management and Budget

OSTP
White House Office of Science
and Technology Policy

RPA
Regional Plan Association

VAI
Van Alen Institute

Credits

Too Big was written and conceived by Henk Ovink and Jelte Boeijenga. The following people have made important contributions to this book:

Interviews With
Laurel Blatchford, Matthijs Bouw, Terrence Brody, Amy Chester, Scott Davis, Shaun Donovan, Marc Ferzan, Carrie Grassi, Bjarke Ingels, Klaus Jacob, Marilyn Jordan Taylor, Eric Klinenberg, Carlos Martin, Marion McFadden, Vincent Mekles, Kate Orff, Daniel Pittman, Damaris Reyes, Judith Rodin, Jeremy Siegel, Jamie Springer, Georgeen Theodore, David Van der Leer and Dawn Zimmer

Special Thanks to
Adri Duivesteijn, Dirk Sijmons, George Brugmans, Han Meyer, Jeff Goodell, Rob Lane, Rob Pirani, Shaun Donovan, Tom Scholten, the Regional Plan Association and Amy Chester and the Rebuild by Design team

Translations
John Kirkpatrick and Harlan "Hal" Clifford

Text Editing
Harlan "Hal" Clifford

Copy Editing
Brannan Sirratt

Design
Koehorst in 't Veld, Rotterdam

Portraits Interviewees
Rachel Sender

Lithography and Printing
Die Keure, Bruges

Production
nai010 publishers, Rotterdam

Publisher
Eelco van Welie, nai010 publishers, Rotterdam

This publication was made possible through generous support from and contributions by: Ministry of Infrastructure and Water Management, Arcadis, Creative Industries Fund NL, Dutch Water Authorities, Van Eesteren-Fluck & Van Lohuizen Stichting, Netherlands Water Partnership, Royal HaskoningDHV, The Rockefeller Foundation, World Water Academy

nai010 publishers is an internationally orientated publisher specialized in developing, producing and distributing books on architecture, visual arts and related disciplines. www.nai010.com

nai010 books are available internationally at selected bookstores and from the following distribution partners:

North, South and Central America - Artbook | D.A.P., New York, USA, dap@dapinc.com

Rest of the world - Idea Books, Amsterdam, the Netherlands, idea@ideabooks.nl

For general questions, please contact nai010 publishers directly at sales@nai010.com or visit our website www.nai010.com for further information.

Printed and bound in Belgium

ISBN 978-94-6208-315-8

Also available as an eBook (PDF): ISBN 978-94-6208-331-8

Photo Credits

AIA New York | Center for Architecture: p. 88; Andrea Booher/FEMA: p. 73; ANP REUTERS/Larry Downing: p. 26; BIG Team / Rebuild by Design: pp. 197, 198, 216; Cameron Blaylock / Rebuild by Design: pp. 122-123, 124, 132, 136, 138, 149, 242-243, 246, 247; Governor's Office/Tim Larsen: pp. 18-19; HR&A Advisors with Cooper, Robertson & Partners Team / Rebuild by Design: p. 182; https://beeldbank. rws. nl, Rijkswaterstaat / Joop van Houdt: p. 29; IBTimes: p. 24-25; Interboro Team / Rebuild by Design: pp. 187, 214; Liz Roll/ FEMA: pp. 6-7; Master Sgt. Mark Olsen/U.S. Air Force, via Associated Press: pp. 44-45; MIT CAU, ZUS and De Urbanisten Team / Rebuild by Design: pp. 147, 179, 210; OMA Team / Rebuild by Design: pp. 200, 204-205, 215; PennDesign/ OLIN Team / Rebuild by Design: pp. 207, 176-177; Rebuild by Design: pp. 135, 153, 180, 203, 206; SCAPE Team / Rebuild by Design: pp. 184, 185, 208-209; Spencer Platt / Getty Images: front cover; WB unabridged with Yale ARCADIS Team / Rebuild by Design: p. 194; WXY/West 8 Team / Rebuild by Design: pp. 193, 212-213

Maps

Hurricane Sandy Surge Extent: FEMA Modeling Task Force Base Map: OpenStreetMap, National Land Cover Database (NLCD) 2011, U.S. Census Bureau.

The Meadowlands

Hunts Point

Lower Manhattan

Hoboken

Nassau ———

Red Hook

Staten Island

Rockaway Beach

Union Beach

Asbury Park